LOUIS ARMSTRONG

by SANDFORD BROWN

An Impact Biography

FRANKLIN WATTS
New York
Chicago
London
Toronto
Sydney

To Claire, my musical Bear

Photographs copyright ©: Archive Photos, NYC: frontis, p. 14 (Central Press); Culver Pictures, Inc.: pp. 1, 2, 4, 15; Hogan Jazz Archive, Tulane University: pp. 3, 16; The Bettmann Archive: pp. 5, 6, 10; AP/Wide World Photos: pp. 7, 8, 11, 13; UPI/Bettmann Newsphotos; pp. 9, 12.

Library of Congress Cataloging-in-Publication Data

Brown, Sandford.
    Louis Armstrong : swinging, singing Satchmo/ by Sandford Brown.
      p.   cm.—(An Impact biography)
    Summary: Examines the personal life and musical career of the famous jazz trumpeter and singer known as Satchmo.
    Includes bibliographical references and index.
    ISBN 0-531-13028-2
    1. Armstrong, Louis. 1900-1971—Juvenile literature. 2. Jazz musicians—United States—Biography—Juvenile literature. [1. Armstrong, Louis, 1900-1971. 2. Musicians. 3. Jazz. 4. Afro -Americans—Biography.] I. Title.
ML3930.A7587 1992
781.65'092—dc20
[B]   92-43192 CIP AC MN

CONTENTS

1

THE ROOTS OF JAZZ

The sounds and rhythms of jazz are an inseparable part of life in the twentieth century, deeply ingrained in the feelings and memories of most of us. Yet barely a hundred years ago, these wonderful sounds had never been heard.

Created in the early years of this century by black musicians in the southern United States, jazz was a completely new kind of music that grew out of the black experience in America. For a long time, many people did not take it seriously. They dismissed it as a fad, a jumpy kind of dance music, or as crude music with somewhat disreputable overtones. Jazz was associated with saloons and brothels, since these were the places where it was often played. White people in particular identified it with a black underclass whose position in American society was even more depressed and isolated than it is today.

But jazz endured, and spread across the country and around the world. While jazz performances have seldom made the "Top 40" lists of popular records, the

2   rhythms and tonalities of jazz have deeply influenced all the music of our time, from swing to rock and roll to contemporary classical. The best jazz musicians and singers have the qualities of creativity and style that define true artists. And jazz itself is recognized by most music experts as an art form which is just as worthy of study and respect as the symphonies of Beethoven or the operas of Verdi. Many people consider it the United States' greatest contribution to mankind's artistic heritage.

While jazz was developed in America, its origins are found in the African roots of the people who created it. The black population of the Americas came in chains, kidnapped from their African homelands over a period of 250 years before the U.S. Civil War. They were brought across the ocean by slave traders to be sold into bondage. In British, French, and Spanish colonies of the West Indies and the American mainland, black slaves did the hard, menial work of colonial society—as stoop laborers in the fields, as ditch diggers, road builders, and domestic servants.

Public opinion turned against the slave trade by the late eighteenth century, both in Europe and in most parts of the United States after the new nation declared its independence from British rule in 1776. But the "abominable institution" (as its opponents described slavery) persisted in the southern states, where the landowners depended on slave labor to maintain the plantation-based economy and life-style.

Music was one of the few comforts in the lives of the slaves. In church, they found solace and emotional release by singing spirituals. In the fields or on the loading docks, they sang work songs to ease the drudgery, songs with rhythms that were often tied to the pattern of the work. There were "field hollers," a series of notes of indeterminate pitch which field hands might sing to express their feelings, and there were work songs with words the singers made up as they went along. These could be anything a singer felt like singing about, including insults to white masters or overseers.

There were songs for dancing, songs for weddings, and songs for funerals—always with the human voice as the main instrument, although banjos and crude drums might be used to provide a rhythmic accompaniment. Blacks embellished their vocalizing with African musical techniques that had been passed down for generations: slurs and vibratos, falsetto leaps, series of different notes sung on the same syllable, and cross rhythms in which the melody line diverged from the underlying beat.[1] Some of these same musical devices can be heard in the chants of West African tribesmen today.

Everything had to be learned by ear and passed along without the benefit of written notes. Few slaves could read or write—and even if they had been able to, the standard European system of musical notation could not have accommodated all of the sounds.

The music of the slaves was not purely transplanted from Africa; it was a fusion of African and European musical influences into something distinctly different. The European influence grew stronger after the Civil War, when southern blacks were at least free from slavery, although their economic and social status was still terribly depressed. Black choral groups like the famous Fiske Jubilee Singers began to tour the country as entertainers who supposedly sang authentic black religious songs. But their music became more and more Europeanized as its popularity with white audiences grew. When it was transcribed into European notation in order to be published, off-pitch notes and out-of-tempo rhythms that were awkward to notate tended to disappear.

Work songs and other black folk music inspired the blues, with its characteristic off-pitch tone achieved by

4   adding flatted third and seventh notes ("blue notes") to the ordinary eight-note scale.[2] The typical blues lyric concerned the feelings of a workingman or -woman about love, infidelity, loneliness, or some other aspect of life, and followed certain traditional forms, such as two repeating lines followed by a third line which rounded off the idea.

> Oh I left that man because he done me wrong,
> Yes, I left that man because he done me wrong,
> And ever since I left him, Lord, the night's so long!

While this began as vocal music, black instrumentalists were playing the blues on horns by the last decade of the nineteenth century. By using throat tones, lip vibrato, and a variety of mutes, brass players could "bend" tones to produce blue notes and the coarse sounds typical of blues singing.[3]

Another musical form, ragtime, was developed in the 1890s by black piano players trying to replicate some of the cross rhythms found in African music. They played the notes slightly behind or ahead of the underlying beat, an effect (known as "syncopation" in European music) which can be produced by clapping your hands between your footsteps as you walk.[4] Rags, as the tunes were called, also owed a great deal to march music.

By the late nineteenth century, black musicians were in great demand in bands. They marched in parades, played at picnics or dances, and provided entertainment in saloons and at private parties. They played blues, ragtime, marches, and even selections from operatic overtures.

In some parts of the South, music was considered almost a black profession. Most of the musicians were self-taught, since few music teachers would accept black students. Many of them could play only by ear.

But written arrangements weren't necessary for the new kind of music—jazz—which was beginning to emerge, a music with a foundation in the blues and drawing inspiration from many sources. It was music you could make up as you went along, starting with a basic theme—a familiar tune, say—and improvising variations of harmony and rhythm as the spirit moved you.

More than any place in the U.S., it was the city of New Orleans where the spirit of jazz moved and flourished. Founded by the French some two hundred years earlier, New Orleans at the turn of the century retained a French flavor which blended nicely with a semitropical climate and an easygoing, tolerant approach to life. Its docks bustled with the business of a major seaport and river port, and its bars and bordellos guaranteed visitors the kind of good times port cities are expected to provide.

The strong streak of puritanism in American life in the late nineteenth century had no place here. New Orleans was full of music and dancing year-round, climaxing with the annual Mardi Gras carnival, when the whole city took to the streets for several days of parading and merrymaking. The city was a club joiner's paradise, with hundreds of professional, sporting, social, fraternal, and other "organizations," and music played a part in nearly all their activities.

Like other southern cities, New Orleans had a large black population, which was segregated from the whites. Relations between the races reflected the tolerant, open-minded attitudes characteristic of the city, and segregation here was not as rigid as it was elsewhere in the South.

Much of the music and dancing which saturated city life was biracial. Whites and blacks shared the festivities at Mardi Gras time, though the whites' carnival had its own King Rex while the blacks crowned their

6 own King Zulu. Black bands often played for white dances, and some bands may have included musicians of both races.

The city's black population included many people with black and white ancestry. Just as white citizens of French descent were proud to call themselves "Creoles," a term originated in the West Indies to distinguish native-born people from immigrants rated lower on the social scale, these light-skinned black citizens were known as Creoles of Color.

When a white aristocrat died, his will frequently provided that his part-African mistress and slave should be freed. His children by the same woman were then automatically free. Some part-African children of wealthy whites were given all the advantages the family could provide. Until late in the century, many were treated by white New Orleanians virtually as social equals. The Creoles of Color lived "downtown," in and around the present French Quarter, while other blacks lived "uptown," south and west of Canal Street. The Creoles did their best to maintain their social distance from the darker-skinned blacks.

The Creoles played an important role in the fusion of the musical traditions that led to jazz. Long before the Civil War, black slaves would gather in a park called Congo Square to celebrate their Sunday half-holiday by dancing and chanting to the accompaniment of crude drums, bamboo pipes, and other traditional African instruments. Their tribal cries and voodoo incantations made Congo Square a major tourist attraction until the 1880s, when the Congo Square dances faded away for lack of participants.

Black musicians were now beginning to move beyond tribal memories and to set aside homemade instruments in favor of trumpets, saxophones, and pianos. The sounds of Africa became more and more mixed with European tones. The best players tended to be the Creoles of Color. They could afford the instruments and music lessons which were beyond the reach of other blacks, and they had more exposure to traditional European music. Creole songs, a blend of French music and rhumba rhythms, added sophistication and complexity to the more crude music derived from African tradition.

The laws and customs developed by southern whites to keep blacks "in their place" after the Civil War gradually eroded the special status of Creole blacks. By the 1890s, all of New Orleans's blacks were viewed as Negroes, regardless of social standing or skin tones. And all were subject to the Jim Crow laws, which formalized the breach between the races. Among other things, these laws denied public music instruction to blacks just as it was becoming widely available to whites.[5]

By widening the social gulf between the Creoles of Color and whites, Jim Crow laws closed the gulf which had separated Creoles from other New Orleans blacks. This hastened the fusing of black musical talent and probably hardened the determination of all black musicians to excel, with or without the benefit of formal instruction.

The Spanish-American War, fought in Cuba in 1898, made a small contribution to New Orleans music. The U.S. Army found itself with a large surplus of band instruments when the war ended, and many of these instruments found their way into secondhand shops in New Orleans, the closest major U.S. port to Cuba. For years after, these shops were a source of inexpensive instruments that even poor blacks could afford.

New Orleans's famous nightlife assured a living for many musicians, who polished their skills playing in the innumerable bars and brothels but earned a meager wage. The city's status as a capital of debauchery

8   had been formalized in 1857, when city officials adopted an ordinance that legalized prostitution and established taxes, licensing fees, and operating rules for the brothel business.

Forty years later, this ordinance was changed to restrict prostitution to one section of town, a section which became known as Storyville after the alderman who proposed the amendment, Albert Story. Storyville was notorious in the years before the First World War for its raucous honky-tonks and dance halls, and for elaborate houses of prostitution called "palaces" or "mansions" or "chateaux." Many establishments had small bands playing the blues for sexually suggestive "slow-drag" dancing or pianists with the durability of human piano rolls who could keep the music going until all hours.

The name "jazz" itself may have come from a slang expression for copulation, though it was not applied to the music until sometime around 1910. "What's called jazz today was called ragtime back then," recalled veteran New Orleans bass player Pops Foster. "From about 1900 on, there were three types of bands around New Orleans. You had bands that played ragtime, ones that played sweet music, and the ones that played nothing but blues."[6]

Much of New Orleans's music was played outdoors in the daytime. Dozens of clubs and other organizations in the city and surrounding towns had their own bands, which would play for picnics, lodge meetings, and carnivals, or assemble anytime on street corners for "cutting" contests that pitted one band against another. These contests were often staged on horse-drawn bandwagons: two bands would pull up in their wagons, open the tailgates, and alternate in playing for the assembled crowd. Each band would strive to win the most applause and thereby "cut" its rival.

Among blacks and Creoles of Color, social clubs often served as "burying societies," a tradition that came from African and other cultures.[7] When a club member died, the club band could be counted on to march at the funeral, playing slow-paced blues on the way to the cemetery and a quick-step march on the way home. "When the Saints Go Marching In" was a favorite post-funeral selection which later became a jazz standard.

In fact, many of the pioneer musicians of jazz developed their techniques in marching bands. The two-beat meter of early jazz reflects the fact that two beats to the measure is the natural rhythm for a two-legged marcher. But variations quickly developed. Instead of playing two slow beats to the measure, musicians would play four beats at twice the speed, sometimes accenting the first and third beats (*boom-chick, boom-chick*), alternating quarter notes with pairs of eighth notes in various patterns (*boom chick-a boom chick-a chick-a chick-a boom boom*), moving between two-quarter and four-quarter time with an exciting rocking effect.

Most of the marching bands were brass bands, with cornets or trumpets as the dominant solo instruments and tubas, trombones, French horns, and other brass instruments helping the drums supply the rhythmic background. Not surprisingly, the star instrumentalists in the early days of jazz were the trumpeters. The trumpet (or its shorter French cousin, the cornet) was the loudest and most brilliant of the brasses and could carry the melody high and clear above the rest of the band.

The first of the great stars was Charles ("Buddy") Bolden. Born in New Orleans in 1878, Bolden grew up in the middle of the brass-band craze. He learned to play the cornet as a youth and also picked up musical ideas in church, where he was a member of a

10   gospel-shouting (singing) congregation. He organized the first real jazz band in 1900, with a cornet, clarinet, trombone, violin, guitar, string bass, and drums. The band worked in saloons, parades, parks, and at private parties; they played polkas, quadrilles, ragtime, and blues—all by ear.

Bolden himself became legendary for his powerful cornet playing. It was said that he could announce a band concert simply by standing on a street corner and sounding a few notes; people would hear him more than a mile away and come flocking to the scene. Old-time New Orleans guitarist Danny Barker believed the city's natural acoustics helped explain this astonishing carrying power. "There was water all around and also water all under the city, and there was the heat and humidity of the swamps, of the bayous all around. And because of all this, because sound travels better across water, when you blew your horn in New Orleans—especially on a clear night—the sound carried."[8]

Bolden blended the African-American rhythms of ragtime with brass-band music, plus the wavering "blue" tonality of southern black folk music. Describing the scene at an uptown dance hall where Bolden played, one author wrote:

"At night . . . the Tin Type trembled with life and activity, especially when Bolden was 'socking it out.' The 'high class' or 'dicty' people didn't go to such low-down affairs as the Tin Type dances. At about twelve o'clock, when the ball was getting right, the more respectable Negroes who did attend went home. Then Bolden played a number called 'Don't Go Away Nobody' and the dancing got rough. When the orchestra settled down to the slow blues, the music was mean and rough, as Tin Type roared full blast."[9]

Another trumpet star was William ("Bunk") Johnson, who could not match Bolden's fiery power but proba-

bly had a greater influence on future trumpeters. Bunk   **11**
Johnson played with a lighter, more subtle touch, antici-
pating the beat or delaying behind it and hurrying to
catch up.

The music of uptown musicians like Bolden and
Johnson was not popular with the older generation of
Creole of Color musicians. As Creole violinist Paul
Dominguez said: "See, us downtown people, we
didn't think so much of this rough uptown jazz until we
couldn't make a living otherwise. If I wanted to make a
living, I had to be rowdy like the other group. I had to
jazz it or rag it or any other damn thing. Bolden
caused all that. He caused these younger Creoles . . .
to have a different style altogether from the old heads
like Tio and Perez. I don't know how they do it. But
goddam, they'll do it. Can't tell you what's there on
the paper, but just play the hell out of it."[10]

Before the twentieth century was very old, many of
those younger Creoles of Color would establish themselves as pioneers of jazz: saxophonist Sidney Bechet
and banjoist Johnny St. Cyr, trombonists Honore
Dutrey and Edward ("Kid") Ory, clarinetists Barney
Bigard and Alphonse Picou, cornetists Freddie
Keppard and Oscar ("Papa") Celestin, and pianist
Ferdinand Joseph ("Jelly Roll") Morton. And other New
Orleans musicians would make a powerful contribution,
such as Joseph ("King") Oliver, whose nickname acknowledged his supremacy among cornetists in his
day. While few whites had much exposure to jazz at
the time, the generation of New Orleans musicians
who came of age with the century included a few out-
standing white jazzmen, such as trombonist George
Brunis and the legendary clarinetist Leon Rappolo, who
flourished in the 1920s before his premature death.

The greatest jazzman of all was born in New
Orleans on August 4, 1901, son of Willie Armstrong,
a laborer, and Mary Ann Albert, known as "Mayann,"

12   a girl of fifteen or sixteen from the Louisiana cane fields. Louis Armstrong's birthplace was a ramshackle house on a dingy street called Jane Alley in the poorest black section of the city.

The building no longer exists, and even the birth date was lost until scholars found it on church records fairly recently. Armstrong always said he was born on July 4, 1900. He probably didn't know his real birthday, since birthday parties were not a part of his impoverished childhood. Like many blacks in the same situation, he chose the nation's birthday to celebrate as his own. Why he added a year to his age is uncertain. It may have helped him find work as a boy, or it may be simply that 1900 seemed like a good year to begin.

Louis grew up without a father—Willie Armstrong abandoned the family shortly after Louis's birth—and he started working when he was seven to help support his mother and baby sister. Music was his joy and the center of his life from the start. He played his first tunes on a toy tin horn and bought his first cornet in a pawnshop when he was eleven. Before he was twenty, he was playing horn with a brilliant inventiveness that amazed his professional peers.

Over the next fifty years, as player, singer, bandleader, and show business personality, he did more than anyone to turn the music of the black ghetto into an American art form and to carry its exhilarating message to the world.

2

A NEW ORLEANS BOYHOOD

The neighborhood around Jane Alley was not the Old South of magnolias and moonlight celebrated in romantic ballads. Located about a mile west of Storyville, near the present intersection of Perdido and Liberty streets, it was so full of violence and vice in the early 1900s that it was known as the Battlefield. The people who lived there were the poorest of the poor, the downtrodden blacks whom other blacks looked down on. They lived in shabby row houses, amid dirt and disease, with never enough food, never enough clothes, and, it seemed, never enough of anything.

To be born and grow up here was to have the odds against you from the beginning. Louis Armstrong's harsh boyhood left a mark he never entirely forgot. Insecurity dogged him all his life; decades later, when he was wealthy and famous, he would show enormous gratitude for even small favors like a limousine ride or a restaurant meal a concert promoter might offer. Yet he confounded the odds. He emerged from a brutalizing environment which turned many of his

14   boyhood friends into criminals and hard cases, to become a man full of love, good humor, generosity, and a relish for life.

Luck played a part. Louis was lucky to have a loving mother and grandmother who did their best to make a chaotic and impoverished family life more bearable. He was lucky to live next to the rag dealer who gave him his first job and reinforced Louis's appreciation of friendship and family. And he was lucky to find, in music, a way to his true self.

Mayann Albert was raised in Boutte (pronounced Bout-tee), a tiny rural town about seventy miles west of New Orleans, and came to the city as a teenager in 1900 to seek a better life. Her cousin Isaac Miles, who lived with his wife and children at 723 Jane Alley, found a place for her to live at No. 719. Just as sugarcane cutting had been the only work available to her in the country, Mayann's only choice in the city was to work as a domestic servant in white people's homes. She probably met Willie Armstrong in the city, perhaps at a dance hall, a picnic, or a neighborhood honky-tonk.

A 1901 baptismal register at the Sacred Heart of Jesus Church records that Louis Armstrong, born on August 4 of that year, was baptized by the Reverend J. M. Toohey on August 25. While Louis thought he had been taken to the church by his father's mother, Josephine, a Catholic, it was more likely a white neighbor named Catherine Walker, who, according to the register, cosponsored him with the Reverend Mr. Toohey. In any case, Armstrong, whose own mother was a Baptist, never worshiped in a Catholic church.[1]

When Willie Armstrong walked out shortly after Louis's birth, Mayann decided to leave the baby in the care of his grandmother Josephine. Armstrong wrote later: "My mother went to live in another fast neighborhood, a cheap 'Storyville' section—what I mean by that is the prostitutes did not receive as much pay for their time as the whores did down in Storyville. Whether Mayann was selling fish [working as a prostitute] I could not say. If she was, she certainly kept it out of sight. One thing, everybody from the church folks to the lowest gave her the greatest respect. . . . She held her head up at all times. Nothing excited her. What she didn't have she did without. She never envied no one, or anything they may have. I guess I inherited that part of life from Mayann."[2]

He stayed with Josephine until his fifth birthday, when he was ready to begin school and was returned to his mother at the Jane Alley house. The trip home on a streetcar was one of his earliest memories, because it involved his first brush with Jim Crow. The neighbor woman who accompanied him scolded him when he thoughtlessly sat in the white section of the car. Louis asked her what the signs in the other area said: FOR COLORED PATRONS ONLY. "Boy, don't ask so many questions; sit down, damn it!" she answered.[3]

Mayann gave birth to a daughter while Louis was away, the result of a temporary reconciliation with Willie. Beatrice, known as Mama Lucy, was two years younger than her brother. The family lived in two rooms with only a coal stove for heat and shabby hand-me-downs for clothes. Louis went barefoot much of the time, and his whole wardrobe usually consisted of a single pair of trousers and a couple of old shirts. Their diet consisted mainly of red beans and rice, okra and collard greens, a few scraps of meat once in a while, and sometimes heavy biscuits served with molasses. Mayann would send Louis to the baker shop that sold two loaves of stale bread for a nickel. Sometimes Louis and his friends would raid garbage pails outside markets to pick up a few spoiled potatoes or onions.

Mayann was not much of a cook, but she had firm opinions about laxatives. She would pick dandelions

16   and other grasses along the railroad tracks and boil them to make a physic for herself and the children. "She told Mama Lucy and me, since we have to eat this heavy kind of food because we couldn't do any better, too poor, we will just have to make the best of it," Armstrong remembered. "She said the food you all eat today you must take a good purge and clean your little stomachs out thoroughly. They will keep the germs away. We both gave Mayann our word that we would stay physic-minded for the rest of our lives."[4]

Armstrong did stay "physic-minded," becoming convinced in later years that a herbal laxative called Swiss Kriss was essential to good health and promoting the idea to his friends. "Swiss Krissly Yours" or "Red Beans and Ricely Yours" were closing salutations in many an Armstrong letter.

Young Louis went to school only occasionally, absent as many days as he was in class. But not many schoolboys have to carry the burdens of family responsibility that fell on him. Mayann had boyfriends who came and went, sharing the family's lodgings for a few weeks or a few months. Talking about them in later years, Armstrong referred to them as his "stepfathers." Some of them were kind to Louis and Mama Lucy and some were not. Some of them beat Mayann in drunken quarrels.

Mayann would disappear for days at a time, leaving the children in the care of cousins or neighbors. Even when Louis was a little boy, his mother seemed to count on him as though he were a brother or husband rather than a son.

Once in a while, Mayann would take Louis and Mama Lucy out to Boutte for a short stay with relatives. Louis had happy memories of these country visits, which provided a welcome change from the hard life of the city.

For all Mayann's irresponsibility, Armstrong always **17** felt his mother did a fine job raising him and his sister and never lost his affection for her. "My mother had good common sense and respect for human beings, yeah," he once wrote. "That's my diploma. I was taught to respect a man or woman until they prove in my estimation that they don't deserve it."

His opinion of his absent father was different. "My father did not have time to teach me anything; he was too busy chasing chippies," he said.[5] He felt the same contempt for the men in his neighborhood who neglected their families and preferred carousing to honest work.

At the age of seven, Louis began working for the Karnofsky family, Jewish emigrants from Russia who lived in the black section just a block from Jane Alley. Starting from nothing, the Karnofskys had built up a good business selling coal as well as an assortment of junk they collected on horse-drawn wagons that rambled through the poorer sections of town. Louis got to know them through his friendship with their sons, Morris and Alex.

"I alternated with the two sons," Armstrong recalled. "One went out in the street buying old rags, bones, iron, bottles, any kind of old junk. Go back to the [Karnofsky] house with the big yard, untie the wagon, pile up the old rags in one place, the bottles, bones and the rest of the junk all in separate places. . . . There was enough room for piles of stone coal which the older son, Morris, sold also.

"On the junk wagon with Alex Karnofsky, I had a little tin horn, the kind the people celebrate with. I would blow this long tin horn without the top on it. Just hold my fingers close together. Blow it as a call for old rags, bones, bottles or anything that people had to sell. Kids would bring bottles and receive pennies from Alex. The kids loved the sounds of my tin horn!"[6]

18   After helping Alex in the day, Louis would work evenings helping Morris sell coal for five cents a water-bucketload. The main customers were the prostitutes who stood in doorways around the neighborhood after dark and bought coal to heat their drab and drafty rooms.

At night, Mrs. Karnofsky would often invite Louis to dine with the family, and Armstrong developed a life-long taste for matzos and other Jewish specialties. The visits gave him a look at a kind of family life he had never known. Mrs. Karnofsky taught him to sing "Russian Lullaby," and Armstrong remembered the family singing it "so soft and sweet, then bid each other good night. They were always warm and kind to me . . . something a kid could use at seven and just starting out in the world. When I reached the age of eleven I began to realize that it was the Jewish family who instilled in me singing from the heart."[7]

The Karnofskys were probably the only white friends Louis had as a boy. But a black child in the South of that day soon learned that getting along with white people was essential in a way that had nothing to do with friendship. You would get farther in life if you had a white man to put in a good word for you. If you wanted to avoid trouble, you stayed on the good side of whites and showed respect, even when you didn't feel like it.

There was no civil rights or black power movement to bolster a black who wanted to stand up to whites as an equal—and there were always some whites who delighted in asserting their superior status.

"At ten years old I could see the bluffings that those old fatbelly, stinking, very smelly dirty white folks were putting down," Armstrong said bitterly many years later. "It seems the only thing they cared about was those old-time shotguns they had strapped around them. So they got full of their mint julep or that bad whiskey the poor white trash were guzzling down like water, then when they got so damned drunk they'd go out of their minds, it's nigger hunting time. Any nigger. They wouldn't give up until they would find one. From then on, Lord have mercy on the poor darky . . . they might shoot him down like a dog . . . my, my, my, those were the days."[8]

Around this time, Mayann moved the family to a place on Perdido Street. They lived in one room, with Louis and Mama Lucy sleeping on wooden pallets while Mayann shared her bed with Tom Lee, another family "stepfather." The children liked Tom. "We had a great understanding, especially about sex time," Armstrong wrote later, describing the grunts he and Mama Lucy pretended not to hear in the darkness.[9]

Besides working for the Karnofskys, Louis found time to earn money running errands, cleaning graves in the local graveyard for tips, and singing in a quartet he formed with some friends. The quartet, called the Singing Fools, sang for pennies on the streets, in honky-tonks, and down by the levee on the bank of the Mississippi. The boys would beat on tins and blow harmonicas to draw a crowd, with Louis playing the same tin horn he used on the rag wagon. One boy performed an early form of break dancing, standing on his head on a bean can and spinning himself like a top while the rest of the group cheered him on.

One day, Louis saw a cornet on sale in a pawnshop window for five dollars and decided he wanted it. He began saving fifty cents a week by borrowing from the Karnofskys against future salary, and bought the instrument. "It was all dirty—but it was soon pretty to me," he later recalled. "After blowing into it awhile I realized that I could play 'Home Sweet Home'—then here come the blues. From then—I was a mess and tootin' away."[10]

20   The quartet learned to harmonize so well that professional musicians would stop by to hear them. But Louis was more interested in learning the cornet than singing. Long before he reached his teens, he would take every chance he had to watch the jazz musicians playing outside of the honky-tonks to draw a crowd. He later recalled hearing Buddy Bolden play in front of a place called Funky Butt Hall "in 1905 or 1906," when Armstrong would have been only four or five. There is little doubt that long before his teens, Louis got to hear many of the best jazzmen in New Orleans and to absorb ideas from them.

"On warm summer evenings," writes a jazz historian, "Bunk Johnson would assemble his small band at Buddy Bottler's place in the tenderloin district, and when the music was going hot summon from behind the piano the urchin he knew was hiding there. And Louis Armstrong, in long pants donned for the occasion, would crawl forth, his eyes wide and idolizing. He would take the cornet for the lessons he had slipped away from home to receive. The teacher rapped the pupil's knuckles at each wrong note just as, years before, Bunk's own teacher had 'smacked the cornet right out of my mouth.' Many a night young Louis went home with his fingers sore."[11]

This scene, probably based on Bunk Johnson's romanticized recollections, almost certainly never happened. "I used to hang around Bunk and the other guys," Armstrong later recalled, "but they were too busy to pay much attention to me."[12] The truth is that Louis was more and more frustrated in his desire to learn the cornet, even as music was becoming more and more the center of his life.

He dropped out of school in 1912 and quit working for the Karnofskys in the same year, since he had outgrown the junk wagon job. He smoked his first marijuana cigarette about this time, developing a taste for

"gage," as it was called, which stayed with him for life. **21**
He also began to get into trouble. Celebrating New
Year's Eve with friends in the early hours of January 1,
1913, he borrowed a .38 revolver from his current
"stepfather" on a dare, took it out on the street, and
fired six blanks into the air. A policeman arrested him
for disturbing the peace. After spending a night in jail,
Louis was sent to the Colored Waifs' Home for Boys,
a New Orleans reform school run by Captain Joseph
Jones.

He spent much of the next three years in the Colored Waifs' Home. Periodically sent back to Mayann,
he was returned to the school on at least two occa-
sions for stealing newspapers from the white boys who
sold them on streetcars. (This was a "whites only" job,
and whenever Louis was seen leaving a streetcar with
papers under his arm, he was arrested.)

Being sent to the Waifs' Home turned out to be
one of the lucky breaks that helped steer Louis's life in
the right direction. Captain Jones, a black man and a
former cavalry officer, was famous among southern
educators for his no-nonsense approach to discipline
and his ability to instill a sense of self-esteem in his
young charges. He organized the school along mili-
tary lines and drilled the boys with wooden rifles. But
the general atmosphere was "more like a boarding
school or a health center than a jail," as Armstrong recalled it. Louis took to the discipline and to the school's
good, nourishing food, putting on weight as soon as
he left home.

The school offered vocational training in carpentry,
gardening, and music, three occupations which offered
plentiful job opportunities to young black men. The music
teacher, Peter Davis, gave individual instruction and also
supervised the school orchestra, a mostly brass band of
some two dozen pieces. Louis started in the vocal chorus, and was then assigned to play tambourine. His

22   sense of timing impressed Davis, who switched him to drums. After a short time, he was switched to alto horn, an instrument resembling a cornet but lower in register. Louis was happy with this move. "I had been singing for a number of years," he recalled later, "and my instinct told me that an alto takes a part in a band same as a baritone or tenor in a quartet."[13]

When an opening developed for school bugler, Louis got the assignment. He was very proud to be selected to play taps at lights-out each night, and worked hard to develop a strong *embouchure* (the way a brass player applies lips and tongue to the mouthpiece of the instrument). Louis cut grooves in the mouthpiece so it wouldn't slip off his mouth, and practiced whenever he could. Davis gave him lessons on the cornet, which calls for the same embouchure as the bugle. He also taught him the importance of producing a good, rich tone on the cornet, a lesson Louis learned well.

While Louis could not read music, Davis quickly came to realize that he was a natural musician of extraordinary talent and made him the leader of the band, a juvenile version of the many jazz bands that played in New Orleans. Louis and his schoolmates played at funerals and basket parties, and marched through the city's streets and parks taking up collections for various good causes. The teacher grew fond of his pupil, who was always good-natured and eager to please. Davis would occasionally take Louis home on his day off and allow him to play duets and sing hymns with his niece Ida, who played the piano.

Louis left the Waifs' Home for good at the age of sixteen, when he was sent to live with his father at the latter's request. Willie Armstrong needed Louis to baby-sit the children from his second marriage while Willie and his wife worked. But Louis was not happy with this situation, and he soon returned to Mayann and Mama Lucy.

At this point, he was fully grown to his adult height **23** of five feet four inches. He was unschooled in spelling and grammar, but he had a natural ear for language and could express himself clearly and vividly. He still didn't read music very well, but he was already a fairly accomplished horn player.

Determined to become even better, he began hanging around the honky-tonks where the best bands were playing. A shy and timid boy who did his best to avoid the violence that was part of life in "the District" (as locals referred to Storyville), Louis was fortunate to befriend a man called Black Benny Williams. Williams, a bass drummer and a pimp who was known for his toughness, would walk through a bad neighborhood with a .45 and take guns away from people to resell for fifty cents or a dollar. "He was devilish and everybody loved him," said Armstrong.[14] Until he was shot by one of his prostitutes, Williams acted as Armstrong's protector in a dangerous world. No one would pick on the boy when Black Benny was around.

Louis was captivated by the sounds of jazz. The band jointly led by the great cornetist King Oliver and trombonist Kid Ory seemed to open up a whole new world of musical ideas to him. And Oliver noticed the boy's interest. One evening, he offered to give Louis cornet instruction if he would come to the Oliver house now and then to help Mrs. Oliver with errands.

While Peter Davis had instructed Louis in the basics of horn playing, Oliver taught him to play jazz. From Oliver, Louis learned techniques of fingering and breath control; he learned how to shape a phrase or bend a note for more dramatic effect, and how to play background for singers or other instrumentalists. While the style Louis developed was quite different from Oliver's, the older man's influence was critical in shaping the young jazz genius. Years later, Armstrong recalled: "Joe Oliver taught me more than anyone. He

24 took up his time with me. Joe used to call himself my stepfather because I was like a son to him, he said. He sure acted like a father to me."[15]

He began to sit in on cornet with local bands, helped by Oliver's recommendations. His first paid job (or "gig" as jazzmen call it) was at a honky-tonk called Matranga's. He found other work in and around Storyville, playing horn for a dollar twenty-five a night plus tips, and began to make a name for himself among local musicians.

Oliver would occasionally have Louis substitute for him in the Ory/Oliver band. In 1917, Louis and a drummer named Joe Lindsay teamed up to organize their own six-piece jazz band. They landed numerous gigs, thanks to Oliver, who threw them any extra work that came his way.

But Louis wasn't earning enough from music to live on. To supplement his income, he took a job driving a mule-drawn coal wagon during the day—grueling, dirty work which involved heaving heavy shovelfuls of coal on and off the wagon. Yet for all the demands on his time, shoveling coal in the day and playing gigs at night, Louis was apt to pop up anywhere in town where a parade was forming, playing cornet with astonishing energy and brilliance. He would also take part in street-corner "cutting" contests.

One rival was Henry (Kid) Rena, a trumpeter who had played with Louis in the Colored Waifs' Home band. The story goes that Rena, aiming to cut a trumpeter named Collins who was reluctant to accept the challenge, tied his bandwagon to Collins's so the other man couldn't drive away. But Louis Armstrong had hidden in the bottom of Collins's wagon. After Kid Rena finished, Louis stood up and played a dazzling solo which put the other man to shame.[16]

One night in 1917, Louis was playing at a tough honky-tonk catering to longshoremen when a prostitute tried to pick him up. He was instantly attracted by the slim, brown-skinned girl, whose name was Daisy Parker, and a few days later he married her. "We were both young and giddy," Armstrong wrote in his memoirs. "She was a little skinny but she was cute. She was older than me and more experienced in the tough ways of the tenderloin district."[17] Daisy was also hot-tempered and jealous, and carried a straight razor, which she would brandish at any provocation. The couple soon separated, and Louis went back to live with Mayann. But the marriage did not officially end until a divorce four years later.

In 1918, Oliver left the Oliver/Ory band to move to Chicago, and Ory asked Louis to take the King's place. The offer certified Louis's reputation as the most talented of New Orleans's young jazz players. Besides playing gigs with Ory, Louis doubled with the Tuxedo Brass Band, a parade and party band, and continued his coal-hauling job.

He also registered for the draft. The latest draft call conscripting eighteen-to forty-five-year-olds "fit me just right," he recalled. "I sure was a proud fellow when I could look back there in my hip pocket and feel my draft card, expecting to go to war any minute and fight for Uncle Sam. Or *blow* for him." The fictitious 1900 birth date qualified the seventeen-year-old Louis to go to war, and enabled him to work in cabarets which would not hire anyone under eighteen.

But Armstrong was still a civilian when the Armistice arrived in November 1918. He was now finally making enough money from music to support himself and help support Mayann and Mama Lucy. The day the war was over, he quit his coal-hauling job. As he recalled it: "I dropped my shovel, slowly put on my jacket, looked at Lady [his mule] and said 'So long my dear, I don't think I'll ever see you again!'"[18]

3

RIVER LEADING NORTH

The wartime economic boom brought big changes for American blacks and for the jazz music that was still almost their exclusive pleasure. Attracted by plentiful jobs in northern cities, hundreds of thousands of southern blacks cut their ties with the South and its oppressive traditions and moved to places such as New York, Chicago, and Detroit. They missed good music in their new lives (phonograph records were still fairly rare), which ensured audiences for the jazzmen, like King Oliver, who followed them north. This exposed more and more white people to the new music and began to build a mass audience for jazz.

The most enthusiastic jazz fans were people in their twenties and thirties—a generation in full rebellion against the customs and life-styles of its elders. They wanted to throw out the stuffy nineteenth-century past, including its music, and jazz had the novelty and slightly illicit flavor to appeal to them. They also wanted to dance. The enthusiasm for jazz was accompanied by a mania for ballroom dancing which

28   saw dance halls springing up all over the country, providing more employment for musicians.

In New Orleans, the exodus of musicians to the north was accelerated when the U.S. Navy Department closed down Storyville. The Navy invoked its wartime powers to board up the bawdy houses of the red-light district in November 1917, labeling them a threat to the health and safety of the numerous sailors taking shore leave in the city. Even though most of the places that employed jazz musicians were not actually in "the District," the Navy's action had a chilling effect on the whole New Orleans scene. It seemed as though a long carnival had ended and the center of action had moved elsewhere.

Oliver had left the Oliver/Ory band for Chicago to join a band led by clarinetist Lawrence Duhe. For Armstrong, the invitation to take his idol's place was irresistible. He began sitting in twice a week with Ory, playing Sundays at a honky-tonk called Pete Lala's and Mondays at a dance hall called Co-operative Hall, while continuing to play with the band at Tom Anderson's and to accept private gigs with other groups. "It was kicks," Armstrong recalled. "Playing Oliver's cornet parts made me feel important."[1]

One night in 1919, a pianist named Fate Marable dropped into Co-operative Hall to hear the Ory band. Marable led a jazz band aboard steamboats that cruised the Mississippi River from New Orleans as far north as St. Paul, Minnesota, well over 1,000 miles (about 1,500 km) upriver. At each port along its route, Marable would play jaunty tunes on the steam calliope (an instrument resembling the organ) to announce the boat's arrival. The sound was guaranteed to draw crowds to the dock, where tickets were sold for an evening excursion. During the cruise, the jazz band would play on the upper deck for dancing.

When Marable heard Armstrong's cornet, he decided he had to have him on the steamboat. Louis accepted the offer, and quit the band at Tom Anderson's to begin work aboard the steamer *Dixie Belle*. For the next three years, he spent most of his time working with Marable on the boats while continuing to do cabaret dates with the Kid Ory band in the city. At first, his steamboat gigs were brief excursions out of New Orleans. But in April 1920, the *Dixie Belle* left its Canal Street wharf for a seven-month trip to St. Paul and back, with a six-week stop in St. Louis to do local excursions.

Louis enjoyed the constantly changing scene during his first real trip away from home. He found a valuable friend in band member David Jones, a well-trained musician who played the mellophone (a large brass horn). "It was Davey who really taught me to read music," Armstrong said. "He used to say 'Louis, you can blow and you can swing because it's natural for you. But you'll never be able to swing any better than you already know how until you learn to read.'"[2] The twelve-piece band also included drummer Warren (Baby) Dodds and banjoist Johnny St. Cyr, New Orleans musicians who would play many gigs with Armstrong later in his career.

In some southern towns where the steamboats docked, many of the white inhabitants had never seen a black band nor heard New Orleans jazz. Marable was doing his bit to break down the rigid color barriers in jazz. As Armstrong said later, "the ofays [white people] were not used to seeing colored boys making fine music for them to dance by."[3]

White jazzmen were still relatively rare, although their numbers were increasing. In Davenport, Iowa, the home port for the steamboat line, a young white trumpeter named Bix Beiderbecke came aboard to catch the Marable band and talk to the musicians. Armstrong

30   met him and recalled him as a "nice kid."[4] It was 1920, and Bix was a high school student unknown outside his hometown. He went on to become a jazz legend—the first white jazz superstar—before his premature death little more than a decade later.

Jack Teagarden, a white trombonist from Texas, was only sixteen when he first met Armstrong on a trip to New Orleans in 1921. Teagarden described the meeting: "In the small hours, a friend and I were wandering around the French Quarter when suddenly I heard a trumpet in the distance. I couldn't see anything but an excursion boat gliding through the mist back to port. The boat was still far off, but in the bow I could see a Negro standing in the wind holding a trumpet high and filling the night with the hottest, the sweetest, the purest jazz I'd ever heard. . . . I stayed absolutely still, just listening, until the boat dropped anchor. . . . I talked to the musicians, and when they landed, Fate Marable presented me to the unknown cornetist with the round, open face: Louis Armstrong."[5]

Teagarden and Armstrong eventually became good friends, and played many cabaret and recording gigs together in the 1940s and 1950s after both had become famous. As Armstrong said after Teagarden's death in 1964, "He was from Texas, but it was always: 'You a spade and I'm an ofay. We got the same soul. Let's blow'—and that's the way it was."[6]

Louis's ready smile and engaging manner made him a popular addition to the steamboat band. He addressed his colleagues as "Pops," "Daddy," or "Face," and used the same names for most casual male acquaintances, seldom standing on formalities. Good jazz, or anything he approved of, was "mellow" or "solid," terms Armstrong may have coined and certainly helped to popularize.

Louis himself—"Li'l Louis" to Oliver band members when he was a worshipful fourteen-year-old hanging

around to watch them play—acquired many other
nicknames through the years. Most of them were
based on his outsize "chops," or mouth. "Every time I
looked around, somebody in some band had laid a
new name on me," he said. "Hammock Face" and
"Rhythm Jaws" were two of the more obscure ones he
recalled; "Dippermouth," "Dipper," or "Dip,"
"Gatemouth" or "Gate," and "Satchelmouth" or "Satch"
were others he heard more frequently. A British journalist unwittingly corrupted the latter into Satchmo during
an Armstrong tour of Europe in the 1930s, and it was
this nickname (which Armstrong loved) that caught on
with jazz fans. To his fellow jazzmen, however,
Armstrong was always "Pops," partly because of his
own addiction to the term, and also perhaps because
he was everyone's senior in jazz talent.

Armstrong's jovial, outgoing nature also registered
on the people who listened and danced to his music.
While strictly a horn player and not yet the singer he
later became, his personality was an important part of
the impression he made on audiences. His love of the
music and the huge pleasure he took in performing
showed in his face. His whole being seemed to com-
municate these feelings, enhancing the golden sounds
that emerged from his cornet.

On the boats or back in New Orleans,
Armstrong's cornet playing was creating a sensation.
He combined the power of Buddy Bolden with the
tonal subtlety of Bunk Johnson or King Oliver. Louis had
learned to read—to "cut the book," as musicians
say—but it was his ability to improvise marvelous melodic phrases which made him stand out, and made
everyone else in the band play better. On fast numbers, no band could help but swing with Armstrong's
horn driving it forward. Where other horn players
slurred or half-tongued, Armstrong hit every note with
a clean, sharp front edge. On long-held notes, he

32   would deliberately start slightly flat and pull up to true pitch the way folk singers did, creating great tension and emotion. He played high notes with more smoothness and clarity than any horn player had ever achieved. As one critic observed, "Armstrong brought high register playing into jazz."[7]

In 1922, Oliver decided to add a second cornet to the band he was now leading in Chicago. He telegraphed Armstrong asking him to come north, and Louis immediately wired his acceptance. "Wasn't nobody going to get me to leave New Orleans but King Oliver," Armstrong said later. "His calling for me was the biggest feeling I ever had musically."[8]

Just before leaving New Orleans, he played a gig at Pete Lala's, where an old acquaintance named "Slippers" stopped by the bandstand to say farewell. A big, tough black man who was usually armed, he had been the bouncer in a honky-tonk where Louis had worked as a teenager. Slippers admired Louis's playing and had looked after him. "When you go up north, Dipper," he told Armstrong as he shook his hand, "be sure and get yourself a white man that will put his hand on your shoulder and say 'This is my nigger.'"[9]

Such advice would sound strange today, particularly coming from a fearless character like Slippers. But this was long before ideas of black liberation and black pride came into their own. The advice made sense in 1922, when a black man's chance of getting ahead more often than not depended on having a white man put in a good word for him. In any case, Armstrong never forgot it. More than a dozen years later, when he signed up with Joe Glaser, an honest, shrewd agent who took charge of the business side of his career, Armstrong felt he had finally met the white man Slippers was talking about.

Louis put on his best clothes—a brown box-back coat, a straw hat, and tan shoes—and, carrying a

straw suitcase containing his cornet and all his other   **33**
belongings, boarded the train. He also took along a
"big trout sandwich" Mayann had fixed to see him
through the long journey. "Son, you got a chance," his
mother told him. "Don't waste it."[10]

When he arrived at the Chicago station he found
no one to meet him and almost went back on the next
train. But he was soon located by a porter Oliver had
left word with. The porter guided Armstrong to the
Lincoln Gardens Cafe, a large dance hall on the South
Side where Oliver's Creole Jazz Band was playing at
that very moment.

The Oliver band was already famous among Chicago musicians when Armstrong joined it. All but one
of its members were New Orleanians Armstrong had
already heard or actually played with: Oliver, trombonist Honore Dutrey, bassist/banjoist Bill Johnson, and
the Dodds brothers—Johnny on clarinet and Baby on
drums. The pianist, a Californian named Bertha
Gonsoulin, would soon be replaced by a woman from
Memphis named Lil Hardin.

The band sounded so good to Armstrong that first
night that he didn't think he could play with it. When he
made his official debut the next night, however, it was
clear to everybody that "Li'l Louis" belonged. "The first
number went down so well we had to take an encore,"
he wrote later. "That was the moment Joe Oliver and I
developed a little system whereby we didn't have to
write down the duet breaks."

The system depended on Armstrong's natural ability
to improvise a perfect second part or harmony to any
melody line. Oliver would lean over to Armstrong while
the rest of the band was playing and move the valves
of his horn to the notes he had picked for his next break.
Knowing what was coming, Louis would make up the
second part and blend in perfectly. To listeners, the im-

34   provised harmony seemed miraculous, like some sort of musical telepathy.[11]

The Creole Jazz Band played ensemble music so closely organized that it could almost be called arranged, although the band members paid little attention to their music sheets (when there were any) since everyone knew each tune intimately. The band would move along in perfect unison, all instruments involved in collective interplay, and periodically stop to let one instrument solo for a few bars. More often than not, the "solo" break would be for two cornets. "Then Joe and Louis stepped out," wrote one observer, "and one of their breaks came rolling out of the two short horns, fiercely and flawlessly."[12]

Imagine the shouts of pleasure that rose from the crowd when that happened! The Lincoln Gardens dance floor and balcony held more than a thousand people at full capacity. Audiences were multiracial and came from all walks of life, although it was predominantly a "sporting" crowd heavily salted with musicians and entertainers. To northern musicians, black or white, New Orleans bands played jazz the way it was supposed to be played—and no band did it better than Oliver's.

A young Indianan named Hoagy Carmichael, later to become famous as a jazz pianist, singer, and composer of such tunes as "Stardust" and "Georgia on My Mind," was nightclubbing with Bix Beiderbecke and another jazzman named Bob Gillette when he first heard the Oliver band's new second cornet. When Armstrong "slashed into 'Bugle Call Rag,'" Carmichael recalled, "I dropped my cigarette and gulped my drink. Bix was on his feet, his eyes popping. Louis was taking it fast. Bob Gillette slid off his chair and under the table. . . . Every note that Louis hit was perfection."[13]

The Oliver band recorded several numbers in

1923 for the Starr Piano Co. under its Gennett label. It **35**
was one of the earliest recording sessions for any
black band. One side, "Chimes Blues," contains the first
trumpet solo recorded by Louis Armstrong. The records, like all others made by black bands at the time,
were intended for distribution to a black audience and
were known in the music industry as "race" records.

The first jazz records, "Livery Stable Blues" and
"Original Dixieland One-Step," were made in New
York in 1917 by a group of five white musicians from
New Orleans who called themselves The Original Dixieland Jazz Band. Their playing was markedly inferior
to that of black bands like Oliver's. ("Livery Stable
Blues" included a trumpet imitating a horse's whinny
and a trombone approximating a moo.) But the record
sold an unheard-of million copies. Within the next few
months, recordings of The Original Dixieland Jazz
Band and other white bands were heard by millions of
Americans on phonographs or on the radio, another
piece of new technology that was rapidly becoming a
fixture in U.S. living rooms. Jazz itself would soon be
transformed from a folk art centered in New Orleans
to a national craze.

It is ironic that jazz won its first great popularity
through white imitations of the blacks who invented it,
though it is not surprising. Far more than today, in the
early 1900s the United States was a white man's
country, with Jim Crow laws still very much in evidence.
Black musicians had to settle for second class in recording opportunities, in concert fees, and even in
hotel accommodations on the road.

When the Oliver band recorded a tune, Armstrong
stood back some fifteen feet from the rest of the group
so his powerful cornet would not overwhelm the other
instruments (including Oliver's) on the primitive recording equipment of the day. Oliver was well aware that
the young star was already surpassing him in talent,

36   although he showed no signs of jealousy and continued to offer Armstrong advice and encouragement. But he did keep the younger man playing second cornet to his lead. This meant Louis had to keep himself reined in—especially since the band's style emphasized instrument blends rather than virtuoso solos.

If this bothered Armstrong, he never showed it. He was happy just to be playing with his musical idol. And Chicago city life was full of wonders. Oliver had arranged for him to live in a South Side rooming house, and Louis was delighted with the accommodations. "In the neighborhood where we lived [in New Orleans], we never heard of such a thing as a bathtub, let alone a *private bath*," he said later.[14]

Getting ready to start a show one night a few months after he arrived, Louis was astonished to see his mother approaching the Lincoln Gardens bandstand. An acquaintance just back from the north had for some reason told Mayann that Louis was sick, had a bad job, and was "hanging his head and crying." She promptly packed her clothes and jumped on a train to see for herself. "When she saw what a fine job I had and how big and fat and healthy I was, she cried," Armstrong said. "She spent the rest of the night right on the stand with us, and we all missed cues and muffed stuff we were so happy."[15]

Mayann had intended to stay for just a few days, but Louis talked her into extending the visit. He took an apartment with her, and bought her a whole wardrobe of new clothes. She lived with her son until winter, when homesickness finally drove her back to New Orleans.

"Big and fat" was an accurate description of Armstrong at that time. He had been putting on weight ever since abandoning hard physical work to play full-time on the riverboats. He was then packing two hundred twenty pounds on his five-foot four-inch frame,

and for the rest of his life he would fight a weight problem, alternately dieting to slim down and ballooning up
again.

His appearance made an unfavorable impression
on pianist Lil Hardin, a college graduate trained in classical music who was three years older than Louis and
far more sophisticated. Having heard musicians describe him as something special, she was disappointed
when they were first introduced in a Chicago cabaret.
She recalled asking other band members, "'How come
you call him Li'l Louis, big as he is?' They said, 'Well,
he's been following us around since he was a little
boy.' I didn't like the way he was dressed, I didn't like
the way he talked, and I just didn't like him. I was very
disgusted."16

Not until she rejoined the Oliver band after an
eight-month absence did Hardin begin to develop
more favorable feelings. Like Armstrong, she was separated after a bad first marriage. The two became
friendly and began "walking out" (dating), apparently
causing considerable jealousy among other band
members. Hardin, a smart dresser with light-brown skin,
"was the Belle of the Windy City at that time,"
Armstrong said. "Who was I to think that a high-
powered chick like Lillian Hardin . . . was stuck on
me?"17

For Louis, Lil was a valuable friend as well as a
lover. She got him to take some weight off by watching
his diet, worked with him to improve his music reading,
advised him on clothes and money matters, and generally helped bolster his self-confidence. In early 1924,
after Mayann made another visit to Chicago to ap-
prove, Louis and Lil divorced their respective spouses
and married.

Even before the wedding, Lil had been suggesting
to Louis that he should think about going out on his
own. Oliver himself had told her that he felt Louis was

38   a better trumpet player than he was. But Louis seemed to lack confidence in himself, especially when Joe Oliver was around. "Whenever Joe came to the house you'd think God had walked in," Lil said. "Louis never seemed to be able to relax completely with him around because he was so afraid of doing something that might upset him."[18]

Only on nights when Oliver was sick did Armstrong get a chance to show his full abilities on the cornet. Louis was also doing a little singing and what he described as "a little comedy dance—I'd slide and fall like I was going to hurt myself." Both the singing and the comedy were popular with audiences, and some band members were openly saying that Armstrong should replace Oliver as leader.

There were other reasons for this rebellion: Oliver was suspected by bandsmen of withholding pay they were owed. The Dodds brothers threatened to beat him up, and Oliver took to carrying a gun for protection. Two saxophonists Oliver added to the band at the request of Lincoln Gardens management began working out duets in an effort to match the cornet duets of Oliver and Armstrong. After an angry Oliver ordered them to stop, the saxmen—Buster Bailey and Rudy Jackson—took revenge by joining Lil in urging Louis to break away. They told him he was wasting his time playing second horn, and that Oliver was past his prime anyway.

Louis would have none of this. "I can't quit Mr. Joe," he told Lil. "Mr. Joe sent for me and I can't quit him." His wife answered, "Well, it's Mr. Joe or me."[19]

In midsummer 1924, while the band was on a six-week tour through the Midwest, Lil, Bailey, and Jackson finally persuaded Louis to make the break. He couldn't bear to tell Oliver to his face, so Jackson broke the news. Oliver must have been shattered, but according to Jackson he took it well. He said he knew Louis was the better player and that he was lucky to have kept **39** him for so long. Oliver even agreed to let Lil stay on as the band's pianist, though he must have known that she had played a big part in Louis's departure.

Armstrong soon landed a job in the Ollie Powers band, then playing a gig at the Dreamland Cafe, which gave him a better chance to let loose the full range of his talents. Then, in the fall, a telegram from bandleader Fletcher Henderson invited Louis to join his orchestra at the Roseland Ballroom in New York City.

It was Armstrong's second job offer from Henderson, who had tried to hire him in 1921 when Louis was working with Marable on the steamboats. Louis had turned down that offer, but he decided to accept this one. In 1924, a chair with Henderson was a place in the big time—or as close to the big time as a black musician could hope to get.

4 THE PEAK OF HIS POWERS

The Fletcher Henderson band was ranked by the black press as the top black band of the day—"not at all like the average Negro orchestra but in a class with the good white orchestras," as one newspaper put it.

A ten-piece outfit when Armstrong joined it, it was an imitation of a white dance band rather than a jazz band. The band played for nightclub and stage shows, recording dates, and occasional road trips in addition to playing dance music (for whites only) at the big Roseland Ballroom in midtown Manhattan. Its repertoire was mainly Tin Pan Alley songs, tangos and waltzes, and somewhat stilted versions of New Orleans jazz.

Henderson, known as "Smack" to musicians, was a skilled leader trained in classical piano. His music was tightly arranged, with emphasis on interplay between the brass, reed, and rhythm sections rather than on solos. Henderson would develop this technique as arranger for the Benny Goodman swing band in the 1930s and 1940s; but even as early as 1924, he

42   was writing fine ensemble arrangements which fore-
shadowed the big bands, assisted by the brilliant
saxman/arranger Don Redman. But his 1924 band did
not "swing." When Henderson sent for Armstrong, he
hoped to add a soloist who could play the kind of hot
jazz the public wanted to hear.

Drummer Kaiser Marshall described the moment
when Louis showed up for his first rehearsal with
Henderson. "The band was on the stand waiting when
he got there, and Louis walked across the floor. He
had on big thick-soled shoes, the kind policemen wear,
and he came walking across the floor, clump-clump,
and grinned and said hello to all the boys.

"He got his seat and opened the book for third
trumpet. Now Henderson had a lot of difficult arrangements . . . and though Louis was a good reader at that
time, he had a little trouble at first. He would make a
mistake and jump up and say: 'Man, what is that
thing?' Then everybody laughed and Louis would sit
down and play it right the next time. . . ."[1]

The orchestrations were annotated with musical expression marks. One time, playing a passage marked
pp (for *pianissimo,* or "very softly"), Armstrong sailed
through at full volume while everyone else was following instructions. Henderson stopped the band and
asked his new trumpeter if he had noticed the *pp.* "I
thought that meant pound plenty," Louis replied, break-
ing up the band with laughter.[2]

It was typical of Louis to relieve the tension with
jokes. But he did have to make a serious effort to brush
up his reading skills. He was rusty despite Lil's efforts,
having had little need for reading with the King Oliver
band.

The other band members were cool to him at first,
except for Buster Bailey, whom Henderson had just
hired from Oliver's band on Armstrong's recommenda-
tion. To Louis, the New York musicians seemed stiff and

stuck-up. They may have been skeptical that Louis **43** could live up to the reputation that had preceded him from Chicago, and may have been put off by his country-bumpkin ways.

As Henderson said, Louis was "a home boy in the big city." Most of the bandsmen were snappy dressers, wearing custom-tailored suits and spats. Most were also habitual night owls who spent their money liberally in the speakeasies (illegal bars) that were the focus of the city's nightlife in the Prohibition years. Louis drank sparingly and tried to save his money; his starting pay of fifty-five dollars a week was apparently less than the other members were making. He took a lot of kidding about his social life and his unstylish clothes, including the long underwear he wore to fend off the cold.

But it wasn't long before Louis's friendliness and playing ability won over the rest of the band—including the other trumpet players, who were the ones most apt to feel threatened by him. His swinging beat and constant stream of new musical ideas inspired the other players to play even better. He also influenced the arrangements written by Henderson and Redman, thus changing the whole style of the band.

According to jazz critic Whitney Balliett, "Louis was the first musician to escape the hidebound four-four beat—through legato flights, behind-the-beat musings and an occasional rushing of the note. With his improvising power and brand-new rhythmic freedom, he not only educated the band, but more important, educated its star performer, Coleman Hawkins." Tenor saxophonist Hawkins, in Balliett's words "a slap-tonguing vaudeville musician" before Armstrong arrived, went on to become one of the greatest saxmen in jazz history.[3]

Jazzmen all over the city reacted to Armstrong as they had in Chicago. Duke Ellington, who had recently organized his own band, said "The guys [musicians] had never heard anything like it." Rex Stewart, a young trumpeter who later became a star with Ellington, said, "I went mad with the rest when Louis hit town. I tried to walk like him, talk like him, eat like him. I even bought a pair of big policeman's shoes like he used to wear. Finally, I got to shake hands and talk with him."

Lil came east for a while to be with Louis, but returned to Chicago when she got an offer to head up her own band at the Dreamland Cafe. Louis missed her, although he was enjoying New York, especially the Harlem nightlife. After finishing an evening performance at Roseland, he and other band members would head up to Harlem to play jazz until three in the morning at a speakeasy for twenty-five dollars apiece. He got a particularly big thrill from being invited to play at the Savoy Ballroom, the famous Harlem showplace that was the ultimate goal of black entertainers.

One time, the band was winding up an evening of dancing at Roseland with "Sugarfoot Stomp," a more polished version of an old blues number called "Dippermouth Blues" that Armstrong had played many times with Oliver. Carried away by the memories, Louis played a solo that had the dance floor pulsating. He suddenly stopped in mid-chorus, shocking the band into silence. He threw his head back, shouted "Oh! Play that thing!" and finished with a rush and a soaring flight into the high register that left everyone gasping. The crowd stormed the stand and actually tried to carry Louis off on their shoulders. Henderson came over to shake his hand—something the unflappable bandleader had never done before.

Henderson later asked Louis what had come over him to make him shout during the break. "I don't know, Smack," Louis said. "It was a break like I used to hear at the Funky Butt when I was a kid. It was that old Perdido cry the folks used to holler at Bolden: 'Oh, Buddy, play that thing!'"[4]

A record of "Sugarfoot Stomp" became a huge seller, which made the Henderson band nationally known for the first time. The cornetist who set the pace, playing the King Oliver blues choruses better than the King had ever done, was not identified on the record label. It was, of course, Louis Armstrong.

Roseland featured a weekly talent show on Thursday nights, when members of the audience would sing or dance or play an instrument. Due to a shortage of contestants, Louis was asked to fill in one night and won first prize singing a song called "Everybody Loves My Baby." He embellished the song with mugging, comic patter, and "scat" singing, in which he substituted nonsense syllables for the words and imitated the phrasing of musical instruments. From then on, the crowd began to call for Armstrong every Thursday night. Later that year, Armstrong made his recorded singing debut with a brief scat break on a Henderson recording of the same song.

Henderson did nothing to encourage his cornet star's vocalizing. Armstrong was seldom allowed to sing on stage, and recorded no other vocals with the band. The best explanation may be that Henderson, a light-skinned, college-educated bandleader who was trying to build his appeal to white mainstream audiences, did not like Louis's gravelly voice. It had echoes of the funky, "disreputable" side of black jazz from which the bandleader was trying to dissociate himself.

Henderson did feature Armstrong's cornet on at least half of the band's records. Louis also got a fair amount of solo time at Roseland, even though the arrangements continued to emphasize section work. He was also in strong demand as a sideman to play cornet on recording dates. While working with Henderson, he independently cut records with blues singers Bessie Smith ("the Empress of the Blues"), and Ma Rainey, saxman Sidney Bechet, and other top artists.

46   Some of these records included Lil Hardin on piano. Lil came east for short visits several times in the next year. While she couldn't watch Louis at Roseland, where only white customers were admitted, she did catch him at rehearsals, and they went nightclubbing at famous Harlem spots like the Cotton Club and Small's Paradise.

Lil complained about being lonely, and was happy to hear that the Henderson band had scheduled a gig in Chicago in the spring of 1925. Louis was also looking forward to the trip and a reunion with his wife and his ten-year-old stepson, Clarence Armstrong. Clarence was the son of Flora Miles, a New Orleans cousin of Louis who had died a few years earlier. Louis had helped bring up the orphaned boy, whose brain had been damaged in a fall, and he and Lil had recently taken Clarence into their Chicago apartment.

But things got complicated. Louis fell in love with a dancer he met at the Cotton Club, a pretty, witty girl named Fanny. Night after night, he would hurry to Harlem after finishing at Roseland to pick Fanny up at the Cotton Club stage door. Then the Chicago gig was canceled, and the Henderson band was booked to spend the summer of 1925 touring the New England states.

For Louis, this meant separation from Fanny as well as not getting home. He did manage to meet Fanny in Boston a couple of times, and rashly promised to marry her if she would only stay, but Fanny had to return to New York. In the meantime, letters from Lil were more insistent: she wanted her husband back home. She missed him as a husband (stories about Fanny may have gotten back to her), and she wanted him in her own band at the Dreamland Cafe in Chicago.

When Henderson's tour ended and the band returned to Roseland, Louis found Fanny had left town. He drowned his blues in a speakeasy and went home

to find a letter from Lil which laid down an ultimatum. **47**
"Take it or leave it," she wrote. "You must choose between Fletcher Henderson and me."

Louis gave his notice next day, ending a thirteen-
month stay with Henderson. His work with the band
had established his reputation with other musicians as a
jazzman of unsurpassed talent, although he was still
not widely known to the general public.

Part of his reason for leaving may have been professional dissatisfaction. Louis was clearly hurt by
Henderson's refusal to let him do more singing. He
was also bothered by the attitude of some Henderson
sidemen, who often played half-drunk and frequently
indulged in musical horseplay, which showed a lack of
respect for the music and the audience. But the main
reason was Lil. Louis had always deferred to her judgment and followed her advice.

A few days after a rousing farewell party thrown
for him by Henderson, Louis joined Lil's "Dreamland
Syncopators" in Chicago on lead trumpet. He was a
big hit, and not long afterwards was offered a job by
Erskine Tate, leader of a fifteen-piece "symphony orchestra" that was playing musical accompaniments for
silent movies at the Vendome Theater. With Lil's approval, he accepted the offer and began doubling
from Dreamland to the Vendome. The Tate band,
which included violins, furnished music for all scenes in
a film, played classical music during reel changes, and
hot jazz numbers at the end of the picture. The piano
player was Earl ("Fatha") Hines, who was beginning to
make his mark as one of the most creative and influential of all jazz pianists. The Vendome gig was the first
of many intersections in Hines's and Armstrong's musical careers.

Tate gave one band member a feature spot each
Sunday. When Armstrong's turn came to solo, he often
played the overture of the opera *Cavalleria Rusticana*

48   and followed with a jazz number. "That's when I could hit fifty high C's or more, maybe pick up a megaphone and sing a few choruses of 'Heebie Jeebies,' or something," he recalled. "It was beautiful. Helped me a lot and got my stage career under way."[5]

Vendome customers began to look forward to Armstrong's feature spots and tried to make sure they didn't miss them. "As soon as the spotlight hit Louis for his feature, man, the people were screaming so much you couldn't hear what he was playing half the time," he recalled Doc Cheatham, a young Chicago jazzman. Cheatham was primarily a saxman at that time, but he switched instruments after seeing Armstrong and began a long and successful career as a trumpeter.[6]

With Louis holding down two jobs and Lil making a good income as the leader on the Dreamland gig, the Armstrong family was becoming fairly prosperous. It was about this time that Louis and Lil rented a house on Chicago's South Side and took Clarence Armstrong in to live with them. Later, when Clarence married, Louis set up the young couple in a Chicago apartment.

Because he was working for his wife at Dreamland, Louis took a lot of kidding from other band members. Sometimes they called him "Hennie," for henpecked, Lil recalled, "because I had too much to say and do about his actions, dress and just about everything. . . . It embarrassed him, and he became hard to get along with at home and on the bandstand. I'd be ready to start the band, and he'd have them off to one side, telling a damn joke. I got after him about it, and he'd say 'Well, if you don't like it, fire me.'"

Years later, Louis wrote: "The guys who called me Henpeck all the time were broke all the time. And I always had a pocket full of money. . . . We were both young, and Lil with the better education and experience only did what any wife would do. . . . Her suggestions were all perfect. I appreciate them all."[7]

When the Dreamland gig ended in early 1926, Louis considered rejoining King Oliver. Lil talked him out of it—he had come too far to take second place to anyone, she told him. Instead, he joined the Carroll Dickerson band, then playing at the Sunset Cafe, while continuing to double at the Vendome with Tate. This reunited him with drummer Zutty Singleton, an old friend from his New Orleans days, who joined Dickerson a few months later.

The Sunset Cafe, which offered a floor show as well as dinner dancing, catered to a mixed black and white crowd. It was owned by Joe Glaser, a shrewd businessman with an eye for talent. When Dickerson left the following year, Glaser appointed Armstrong leader of the band, and billed him in marquee lights as "Louis Armstrong, World's Greatest Trumpet Player." Years later, he would play a much bigger role in Armstrong's career, as his agent and manager.

Armstrong was doing more and more vocals and working out little comedy routines to spice up his "act." He was beginning to think of himself as an entertainer rather than simply a horn player. If he had a model, it was probably Bill "Bojangles" Robinson, the great tap-dancing star he had seen in a vaudeville show several years earlier. "He was the sharpest Negro man that I have personally ever seen on stage," Louis recalled. "His every move was a beautiful picture. . . . He told a lot of funny jokes, which everybody enjoyed immensely. Then he went into his dance and finished by skating off the stage with a silent sound and tempo. Wow, what an artist! I was sold on him ever since."[8]

At the Sunset, Armstrong made the switch from cornet to trumpet, an instrument with more power and brilliance in the upper register. He was at the peak of his powers as a horn player, combining the strength and creative verve of youth with experience developed over a decade of playing with some of the best

50 jazzmen of the day. His energy seemed limitless. Night after night, beginning at 7:00 P.M., he would play four shows at the Vendome, finishing at 11:00 P.M. He would then go to the Sunset to play until three or four in the morning, including time for rehearsing new arrangements. And quantity did not diminish quality. His work rose to heights of virtuosity that set new standards for instrumental jazz.

Of course, much of this music was lost as soon as its echoes died, surviving only in the memories of listeners who happened to be there. Fortunately, Armstrong found time to record. He played on sixteen records cut in 1924 by Clarence Williams's Blue Five, a group whose shifting personnel occasionally included Sidney Bechet and guitarist Charlie Christian, two other jazzmen of the first rank. In the same year, he cut more records as an accompanist for blues singers Bessie Smith and Ma Rainey. And he signed an agreement with OKeh Records to make a series of records as leader of small bands assembled specifically for the recording sessions.

OKeh was a leader in the "race" record market and boasted superior recording equipment for the time. The first records, billed as the Louis Armstrong Hot Five, grouped Louis with four musicians he knew well: Lil on piano, Kid Ory on trombone, Johnny Dodds on clarinet, and Johnny St. Cyr on banjo. During one 1925 session, Armstrong played a brief trumpet chorus on "Heebie Jeebies" and then sang the vocal, reading the lyrics from the sheet music. He was about to start a second chorus, when he dropped the sheet music. Rather than stop the band and start over, he continued to sing without missing a beat, substituting nonsense syllables for the words. "Heebie Jeebies" became the first scat singing hit in record history, selling more than forty thousand copies in a few weeks and giving Armstrong the beginnings of a much wider audience.

On the flip side is "Muskrat Ramble," written by Kid Ory. With Armstrong's horn driving the band, the Hot Five performance established it as one of the most popular jazz tunes of all time. Louis wrote the basic melody for "Cornet Chop Suey" while sitting on a stairway in the recording studio. But its sixteen-bar "stop-time" chorus in which the rest of the band stops playing and leaves the trumpet to carry on alone, is pure improvisation. Louis plays the solo with an exuberant beat and wonderful phrasing—each musical phrase growing out of the previous one and leading into the next, each contrasting with but also related to the others.

Over a four-year period from 1925 through 1928, Armstrong cut sixty-five records for OKeh—a series known collectively as the Hot Fives, though the size and composition of Armstrong's supporting cast changed as some musicians left town for other gigs and others became available for recording sessions. Jimmy Strong, Fred Robinson and Mancy Carr replaced Dodds, Ory, and St. Cyr respectively in some 1926 recordings. The band added Baby Dodds on drums and Pete Briggs on tuba in the same year to record as the Louis Armstrong Hot Seven. The Hot Five in 1928 was actually a sextet, with Earl Hines replacing Lil Hardin on piano and Zutty Singleton taking over the drums.

Louis does some singing on every record of the 1928 Hot Fives, demonstrating the same instinctive gifts for jazz phrasing in his vocals that he does with his horn. And the trumpet solos are among the finest of his career. Musicians still marvel at his trumpet cadenza hitting every note of the chromatic scale in "West End Blues," his rapid-fire triplets and glissandos in "Struttin' With Some Barbecue," his back-to-back trumpet and

52   vocal solos on the furiously swinging "Hotter Than
That," and his stop-time horn chorus following Dodds
and St. Cyr breaks on "Potato Head Blues." In these
and many other peak moments on record, Armstrong's
musical inventiveness is decades ahead of its time.

"His solos were always climactic,—another first in
music," says critic Whitney Balliett. "He would start with
a subtle restatement of the melody, changing its ac-
cents or notes ever so slightly by cutting a phrase short
here or lingering over a note there . . . then, leaving
the melody, he would begin a series of angelic ascen-
sions and swoops that would be occasionally an-
chored by short blue phrases . . . and that would
move up steadily from plane to plane."9

While OKeh had exclusive rights to Armstrong's recorded performances during this period, other companies were pursuing him. The Hot Five recorded two
sides for the Brunswick company in 1926, billing themselves as "Lil's Hot Shots" to hide Armstrong's participa-
tion from OKeh. Louis sang on one number, and his
voice was easily recognizable even though it was part
of a chorus.

The president of OKeh called him in, put the record
on a turntable, and asked: "Do you know who is singing, Louis?" Rising to leave, the flustered Armstrong replied, "I don't know sir, but I won't do it again," as he
disappeared through the door. (In fact, he did make a
few more records for Brunswick with bands fronted by
other musicians, avoiding vocals and apparently even
disguising his horn playing to escape detection.)10

But it was the Hot Fives that made jazz history.
Jazz-record collectors in the 1920s were almost ex-
clusively young, white, and middle class, and they
concentrated on the records of white jazzmen like
trumpeters Bix Beiderbecke and Red Nichols or trombonists Jack Teagarden and Miff Mole. The Hot Fives
broke that pattern, and by 1930 the "colored style" of

black artists like Armstrong, Henderson, and Duke **53** Ellington had caught on among white jazz lovers both in the United States and abroad. In fact, when Armstrong made his first tour abroad in 1932, his first concert broke the all-time attendance record for London's Palladium. "I just couldn't figure out how all those people over there could have come to hear about me, let alone make so much fuss over me," he said. "Pretty soon, I began to understand—they were record fans. Hundreds of thousands of fans, who buy new records as fast as they are made."[11]

Armstrong's heavy schedule of live gigs and recording dates increased his income but left him less time to enjoy it. He and Lil had taken a lakeside cottage at Lake Idlewild outside of Chicago, and Lil, the business brains of the family, also invested in some lakeside lots. Louis enjoyed the first summer at Lake Idlewild, which gave him a chance to do some real swimming for the first time since he had splashed in the Mississippi as a boy. He often swam across the mile-wide lake and back, while Lil, who was afraid of the water, preferred to watch from the shore.

The trips to the lake became rarer as the 1920s drew to a close. "I never had time to be at home except just for a few hours' sleep," Armstrong said. "I met myself coming and going. I guess it was about that time and because of that that Lil and I first started to drift apart."[12]

The truth was that the marriage had never really worked. The couple quarreled frequently and stormily, and every once in a while they would separate, drawing all their money out of the bank and splitting it up. Louis continued to step out with other women, and in 1928 began a serious relationship with a woman named Alpha Smith, who worked as a domestic for a wealthy Chicago family. Alpha was a good-looking, easygoing companion with none of Lil's take-charge

54   personality. Her main talent was for spending Louis's money on furs and other luxuries.

Yet Louis and Lil always remained friends. Lil continued to manage family finances and worry about Louis's career moves, and they continued to work together. Drummer Zilner Randolph recalled them putting on an impromptu show at a theater in the late twenties. "The act was immaculate. They looked like they could breathe together. . . . She was a good dancer. But she didn't do much dancing, just the witty little things she and Louis would do. She would sing, Louis would play the horn. Then they would start ribbing one another."[13]

Louis lost another member of his family, one who was even closer to him than Lil. Mayann came north for long visits in 1925 and 1926, and Louis took pleasure in seeing that she had everything she needed. When she fell ill in New Orleans in 1927, he had her brought to a Chicago hospital, where he felt she would get better care. But Mayann had led a hard life and was worn down though she was only in her mid-forties. After lingering for three months, she died.

Louis arranged a fine funeral and wept as he stood over his mother's coffin—the first and last time he shed tears as an adult, he said years later. He would always present a jolly face to his public. But music critics replaying the Hot Fives detect a deepening emotional quality in his playing and singing about that time, particularly in slow-paced blues classics like "West End Blues" and "Savoy Blues." It might well reflect his grief for a lost time and for the one person in the world who had always loved him.

5

HARD TIMES, NEW DIRECTIONS

Stocks were soaring, business was booming, and the whole country was kicking up its heels as the 1920s drew to a close. The national mood found its sound effects in the hot jazz which filled speakeasies and dance halls and poured from millions of radios and phonographs—instruments which had been rare in U.S. homes a decade earlier.

For Armstrong, it seemed like the best of times. Playing at the top of his form, he was acknowledged to be the best instrumentalist in jazz, and to black Americans he was more than that. While some blacks were embarrassed by the funky jazz traditions he represented, far more saw Louis as a hero, a model, and a hopeful symbol in a segregated society that routinely treated blacks as inferiors. In popular music, white bands got the most attention and money, and blacks almost never got to play head-to-head with whites on the same bandstand. But Louis's exalted status in his profession refuted the whole idea of black inferiority.

56   Unfortunately, the good times were soon to end, for Louis and for most Americans. The Depression would put a third of the nation out of work, and hit the cabaret and theater business hard. While Armstrong seldom lacked a paying gig during this period, it was a time when both his professional and personal life often seemed to be falling apart.

Pushed by agents and promoters, he traveled and performed with hardly a break; overwork, plus his eagerness to please audiences with high-note trumpeting, stressed his lips to the point of breakdown. The bands put together by promoters for his club or record dates were often slapdash outfits that did little to showcase his talents. Rival agents lied to him and cheated him, and he was threatened by gangsters, who had a stake in many clubs where he played. His marriage deteriorated, as he saw less and less of Lil and their quarrels became increasingly violent.

When the Sunset Cafe closed in 1927, Armstrong had a fling at running his own dance hall in partnership with Earl Hines and Zutty Singleton. They opened a place called the Usonia and organized a small band to play there, confident that Armstrong's reputation guaranteed success. But a larger, more lavish club opened nearby with an orchestra led by Carroll Dickerson, and the Usonia went out of business in a few weeks. Louis and Zutty then joined the Dickerson band, staying with it until early 1929.

In March, 1929 Armstrong got a wire from Tommy Rockwell, the recording director for OKeh whom Louis had just signed as his manager. Rockwell, a white man who specialized in supplying black talent to club and theater owners, wanted Louis to front a band led by pianist Luis Russell at Harlem's Savoy ballroom and to also cut some records.

The black fans at the Savoy went wild over Armstrong, whose concerts were broadcast on network radio. The recording sessions, unusual because they teamed Louis with white jazzmen like Jack Teagarden and pianist Joe Sullivan, produced some memorable discs. Some were traditional New Orleans numbers like "Mahogany Hall Stomp," while others were invented on the spot. Because they worked late, the musicians often stayed up all night before appearing for the usual 8:00 A.M. recording sessions. One day they brought a gallon jug of whiskey with them. When the recording man asked for the title of a blues number they had just created, Armstrong looked at the empty container and said: "We sure knocked that jug. You can call it 'Knockin' A Jug.'"[1]

Louis also made some records with the Russell band, the kind of "big band" which would soon dominate the music business. The hit record of this session was "I Can't Give You Anything But Love," on which Armstrong performed trumpet and vocal solos. He was turning more and more to popular songs like this for his material rather than tunes in the black jazz tradition.

Returning to Chicago, Armstrong rejoined the Dickerson band at a new South Side club. But the Chicago cabaret scene was fading in 1929, and the club was unable to meet the band's payroll. When Louis got a telegram from Rockwell urging him to come east again, the whole band decided to head for New York, using Armstrong's name because it was better known in Harlem. Louis divided his available cash to provide twenty dollars for each man, and the group set out in four battered cars, two with vibraphones tied on the roofs.

Hearing his solos on loudspeakers in record stores and cafes along the way, Armstrong became fully aware of how much the Hot Five records and the radio had spread his reputation. When the group visited night spots in cities like Detroit, Cleveland, and Pittsburgh, local jazzmen greeted them as celebrities, in-

58   sisting that they join in jam sessions and picking up their food and drink checks.

Despite this, their money ran out. "We didn't know enough to make stops to play [paid gigs]," recalled Zutty Singleton. "We took our time, and saw the country."[2] The vibraphones rusted en route, and when Dickerson's car was involved in a collision, its passengers had to crowd into the remaining cars for the rest of the trip. The radiator of Louis's car was steaming when he reached Times Square, where he was pulled over by a policeman. Noticing the Illinois license plates and the instrument cases, the cop winked and asked the musicians if they were carrying shotguns (the Valentine's Day Massacre a few weeks earlier had reinforced Chicago's reputation for gangsters and crime).

Expecting only Armstrong, Rockwell was shocked to find an entire band—especially since he had arranged for Louis to play in the pit band for a new musical comedy called *Great Day*. The show, with music by the prominent composer Vincent Youmans, was in rehearsal in Philadelphia. It looked like a hit, Rockwell said, and would give Armstrong a chance to reach a new kind of audience.

After Rockwell promised to try to find work for the other men, Louis went to Philadelphia. Some former colleagues from the Henderson band had also been hired for *Great Day,* but he had barely arrived when the show's music director began replacing Henderson men with white players. Louis was dropped when the director decided he was "not adapted to show business"—surely one of the worst judgments in show business history. The musical flopped on Broadway, despite a good score which includes such standards as "More Than You Know" and "Without A Song."

Armstrong rejoined the Dickerson men for a gig at a Harlem nightclub called Connie's Inn, while doubling in the pit band at the Hudson Theater for a revue called *Hot Chocolates*. His role in the show was strictly **59** as trumpet player at first, but was expanded to include singing the show's top tune, "Ain't Misbehavin'," written by Fats Waller, and a novelty number called "Two Tons of Fun," in which he appeared with Fats and other hefty vocalists.

The show was such a hit that producer Connie Immerman, the owner of Connie's Inn, put on a short version at his club. Louis would finish a performance of *Hot Chocolates* at the Hudson and rush uptown to do the same numbers at Connie's Inn.

When business began falling off in 1930, Immerman fired the whole Dickerson band, including Louis. Rockwell urged him to join Luis Russell at the Savoy. Louis knew his departure would hurt the Dickerson band's chances for new gigs and mean a separation from old friends like Zutty Singleton, but he decided to make the switch.

Armstrong wanted to please the white, middle-class fans who patronized the theaters and nightclubs where he played most of his gigs. He sensed that the old-time honky-tonk jazz, with its shouting, slurred notes, sexual innuendos, and rough improvisations, was no longer the best way to appeal to them—and he was right. What they now wanted was written arrangements of popular songs, played cleanly and smoothly with a pure tone. Sweet music was crowding out hot in the public's musical preferences.

Most of the old-time stars like Oliver, Morton, Bunk Johnson, and Kid Ory failed to adapt to changing tastes and faded into obscurity by the mid-1930s. But Armstrong's fame continued to grow because he gave audiences what they wanted—in his horn playing, his singing, his radiant smile, and his showmanship. Fans screamed approval when he pushed a solo higher and higher, climaxing it with a succession of notes

60   above high C. It didn't seem to matter that such "circus" trumpeting often left little room for jazz feeling.

After a tour of New England with the Russell band, Louis went to Los Angeles, where Rockwell had booked him to play with the house band at Frank Sebastian's New Cotton Club. The club was across the street from the Metro-Goldwyn-Mayer lot, and Louis loved seeing movie stars come in to watch him play. During this gig, he was offered a role in a movie. *Ex-Flame,* a grade-B domestic drama with incidental songs by Armstrong and the orchestra, was the first of many films in which Louis would appear.

One night, during an intermission in the New Cotton Club show, Armstrong and drummer Vic Berton went out to the parking lot to smoke marijuana. As Louis recalled it, "Vic and I were blasting this joint—having lots of laughs and feeling good enjoying each other's company. Just then, two big detectives came from behind a car—nonchalantly—and said to us, 'We'll take the roach, boys.'"[3]

The musicians were allowed to finish the show before they were taken to the police station. On the way, a detective told Louis in confidence that the police had been tipped off by another bandleader, who was jealous of Armstrong's success.

After spending several nights in jail, Armstrong and Berton were tried on a misdemeanor charge and sentenced to six months' imprisonment. Tommy Rockwell dispatched lawyers and a sharp operator named Johnny Collins to try to fix the case, and managed to get the sentence suspended. Genuinely shaken, Louis announced he would never touch gage (marijuana) again.

Jazz musicians laughed when they heard this, predicting—accurately—that Louis would soon resume rolling the cigar-sized joints he loved to smoke. "We always looked at pot as a sort of medicine—a

Louis Armstrong, his sister, Beatrice, and his mother in 1920. Louis was playing at The Orchard Cabaret in New Orleans, earning twenty-one dollars a week.

The King Oliver Creole Jazz Band, which played in Chicago in the 1920s. (Left to right) Johnny Dodds, Baby Dodds, Honoré Dutrey, Louis Armstrong, Joe Oliver, Bill Johnson, and at the piano, Lil Harden

ng's Hot Five,
2h Record Artists.

To Sonny
From
Lou

Standing around the piano are the
Louis Armstrong Hot Five Band, whose jazz
recordings in 1925 made music history.

Louis Armstrong (fourth from left) and his fellow musicians in their tour bus. His manager is second from left.

Louis Armstrong (left) plays with his
Jazz Combo in the 1930s.

Louis Armstrong appeared with the greatest figures of jazz music. (Left) In 1946 he welcomed the incomparable singer, Billie Holiday, to New Orleans. (Above) In 1946, Duke Ellington (at piano) and Louis Armstrong made a recording together of "Long, Long Journey."

The United States government sent
Louis Armstrong on several goodwill tours around
the world as the American ambassador of jazz.
In 1949 he plays in Paris for French firemen,
policemen, and the republican guards.

In this photograph, taken in 1956 in Egypt, Louis Armstrong plays for his wife, Lucille, and the Sphinx.

Three great musical artists in the 1950s:
(left to right) Lionel Hampton, Louis Armstrong,
Dizzy Gillespie.

Louis Armstrong with Ella Fitzgerald

Kwame Nkrumah (right), prime minister of Ghana, welcomes Louis Armstrong and his wife Lucille on the 1956 tour.

During his visit to Africa, Louis Armstrong and his jazz band (at left) are met by African trumpeters (at right) at the Accra airport.

Louis Armstrong and his tremendous talent were an inspiration to children around the world.

Louis Armstrong and friends on the front steps of his home in Queens County, New York City

cheap drunk and with much better thoughts than one **61** that's full of liquor," Louis said later.[4] He considered it no less indispensable than Swiss Kriss, his laxative of choice, and years later wrote a letter to President Eisenhower urging that marijuana be legalized.

Armstrong made some excellent records in California with a band led by Les Hite. His singing and playing on "Shine," a song with a patronizing "good darky" lyric, transforms its material into something deeply moving. "I'm Confessin'" shows Louis adopting a smoother singing style in the tenor range, clearly influenced by the rising star Bing Crosby. (Crosby acknowledged that his own style was powerfully influenced by Louis's phrasing.) "Memories of You" is notable for trumpet and vocal solos by Armstrong and vibraphone playing by the orchestra's young drummer, Lionel Hampton. It was Armstrong who talked Hampton into trying his first solo on the vibes, the instrument that would carry him to fame as a soloist and bandleader.

Both Lil and Alpha Smith visited Louis on the Coast. During Lil's visit, he learned she had been stepping out with someone and resolved to divorce her when he got back east. Lil agreed. "You don't need me now you're earning a thousand dollars a week. We'll call it quits," she said. While the couple didn't bother with a legal divorce for another six years, this was the final parting. Louis made an "alimony" settlement by giving Lil their house and most of the money he had at the time.

He also signed Johnny Collins as his manager after Collins convinced him he had struck a deal with Rockwell to take over Louis's bookings. Collins had booked Louis and a new band at a Chicago club called the Showboat, and Armstrong agreed to the gig.

On the second night of his Showboat engagement, Louis wrote later, "This big bad-ass hood crashes my dressing room and instructs me that I will open in such-

62   and-such a club in New York the next night. I tell him I got this Chicago engagement and don't plan no traveling. And I turn my back on him to show I'm *so* cool. Then I hear this SNAP! CLICK! I turn around and he has pulled this vast revolver on me and cocked it. . . . So I look down at that steel and say 'Weeellll, maybe I *do* open in New York tomorrow!'"[5]

The New York club was Connie's Inn, where, unknown to Louis, Tommy Rockwell had committed him to appear. Armstrong, angered by the club's abrupt dismissal of his band, had no intention of going. But he was caught in a feud between Rockwell and Collins, both of whom probably had gangland contacts. Armstrong and the band slipped out of Chicago and soon left on a long tour of the Midwest and South, accompanied by Collins and his wife and by Alpha Smith.

The climax of this tour was a long engagement at the Suburban Gardens in New Orleans. It was Louis's first visit to his hometown since he had left for Chicago a decade before, and people had not forgotten him. "When our train pulled into the old L&N station, I heard hot music playing," he wrote. "Stretched out along the tracks were eight bands, all swinging together, waiting to give us a big welcome. As soon as I got off, the crowd went crazy. They put me on their shoulders and started a parade down Canal Street."[6]

Banners welcoming Louis were strung across streets, a cigar was named after him and a boys' baseball team played in new uniforms with "Armstrong" emblazoned on the front. Louis paid a sentimental visit to Captain Jones at the Waifs' Home and looked up many other old friends.

The band played to sellout crowds for three months at the Suburban Gardens, a white nightclub just outside the city. Black fans had to stand outside to listen through open windows or tune in to nightly radio broadcasts of the show. On the first broadcast, the **63** white announcer declared, "I haven't the heart to announce the nigger on the radio," and Louis had to come to the microphone to handle the introduction himself.[7] He continued to do this for the rest of the gig, but racism left a sour taste. Except for a 1935 appearance at a black dance hall, he did not perform in New Orleans again until Jim Crow laws were abolished many years later.

The Suburban Gardens gig was followed by a bus tour of a theater chain. In Memphis, a policeman saw a black band member sitting on the arm of the white Mrs. Collins's bus seat and arrested the whole band for violating segregation laws. The theater owner persuaded the police to let them off when the band agreed to do a local radio broadcast. Louis dedicated one tune to the chief of police. The song was "I'll Be Glad When You're Dead, You Rascal You."

Still worried about the Rockwell/Collins feud and the threat of gang violence, Armstrong was happy to get an invitation to leave the country. A British promoter offered a twenty-day gig at the London Palladium, and Louis sailed for England on the liner *Majestic* in the spring of 1932, accompanied by Alpha, Alpha's mother, and the Collinses.

A band which included some black-American jazzmen from Paris was assembled barely in time for the opening. The show drew capacity crowds eager to see the "Colored Trumpet King," as Louis was billed. Another king—George V—was in the audience one night. Louis bowed in his direction before the first tune. "This one's for you, Rex," he said.

While Louis got an enthusiastic reception, his first trip abroad was not a total success. Audiences were not prepared for his clowning, and he seemed crude to many people as he bounced about the big stage wiping sweat from his brow with a handkerchief. Cat-

64   calls and racial insults were shouted from the balco-
nies, and some people walked out. Even musicians
who appreciated the quality of his playing were put
off by his stage antics and showboating.

After a few other gigs in England, Armstrong returned to New York to appear in a revival of *Hot
Chocolates* and record for the Victor company. He
had ended his association with OKeh when the company went bankrupt, and lawsuits resulting from his split
with Tommy Rockwell continued to hang over him.
Collins, moreover, was proving to be a disastrous
manager. In England, he had often been drunk and
abusive and had embarrassed Louis at one point by
refusing to let him go on until the promoter paid in ad-
vance. Back home, he failed to provide the well-
organized, carefully publicized tour and recording
schedule Armstrong needed.

Instead, he worked his client like a mule, accepting
any theater or dance hall gigs that came along. In theater work, a bandleader was expected to put on a
show as well as make music. Armstrong would race
about the stage, executing slides and pirouettes in between trumpet breaks, introducing numbers with mugging and comic patter, and lighting up the theater with
his incandescent smile.

Even playing the run-down dance halls where
Collins booked many one-nighters, Louis was invari-
ably cheery, telling jokes and reaching out to the
crowd. Sideman Scoville Browne recalled: "He would
pick out the seediest girl in the place and come up and
give her a kiss on the cheek. He tried to make everybody feel good. When we would go back to a place
we had been before, he could call 'Hello Joe,' 'Hello
Amos,' 'Hello Percival,' and he hadn't seen any of
these people for a year."[8]

Browne thought the younger players would have
worked for nothing to be with Louis, but the band

eventually went on strike over pay. Collins was prorating salaries according to the number of days actually worked, so that many band members came home from a tour broke. When the strike forced Collins to pay their contracted salaries, the manager angrily canceled further band tours and booked Armstrong for another solo tour of Europe.

While Armstrong himself had managed to save some money, he could have earned far more with good management. He could also have avoided the overwork which was threatening permanent damage to his lips.

Louis was troubled by calluses or scar tissue on the inside of his lips for most of his career. He relied on salves to deal with the soreness, and every few years would remove the calluses with a razor, taking some time off from playing to let things heal. Playing in Baltimore one night in November 1932, he split his lip wide open. He managed to complete his solo on "Them There Eyes," though he was bleeding and every note was agony, sinking to his knees as he strained to finish with his usual F above high C.[9]

But he took little time off to rest. Under pressure from Collins, he was playing again within days, skipping notes and slurring passages to ease the pain. On many of the Victor records, his trumpet tone is noticeably cloudy. At a recording gig in April 1933, Victor had to shorten Louis's choruses and expand other band members' solos to get Louis through, and his pain was evident. But no one (including Collins, who was present) thought to postpone the session.

"Always something would be wrong" with Collins's gigs, Louis recalled years later. "He was always in trouble with promoters—trying to make me declare bankruptcy, mixing me up in stinking publicity stunts, fantastic stuff."[10]

66   Armstrong could have resisted such exploitation, of course. But an insecurity that went back to his childhood made it hard for him to take a stand. He was used to relying on other people to make decisions for him. And he had grown up in a world where blacks did not question the authority of whites, especially aggressive characters like the tough-talking, cigar-chewing Collins. Having put his affairs in Collins's hands, he felt obliged to play whatever gigs he was assigned for whatever the manager wanted to pay.

Along with physical discomfort, Armstrong was burdened in some recording sessions by inadequate backup bands and inferior arrangements. His trumpet work often consisted of a simple statement of the melody at the start and a flourish of high notes at the finish, with none of the improvised variations on the melody that are the essence of his talent.

Yet he continued to make great music. On some records from this time, he plays horn with his typical mellow tone and sharp-edged attack, though his solos are shorter. And his singing is better than ever. His "sweet" tenor was fading as growths on his vocal chords caused a rasp in his voice, but his way with a melody and ability to suffuse a song with tenderness transcended his vocal limitations.

His recordings of "Stardust," "All of Me," "I Surrender Dear," "Body and Soul," "In My Solitude," and "I Gotta Right to Sing the Blues" showed that Louis could improve even a good popular song and, in a sense, make it his own. Another memorable record from that era is "Sleepy Time Down South," which Armstrong decided to make his theme song the first time he heard it.

In the summer of 1933, Armstrong sailed for England again, accompanied by the Collinses and Alpha. Not long after his arrival, Louis found he had bills for money he didn't have. Collins, who was supposed to be paying Louis's taxes and sending money to Lil, had done neither. He had also been paying Louis as little from the proceeds of gigs as he thought he could get away with.

Finally seeing Collins for what he was, Armstrong denounced him and fired him on the spot. Collins stayed around long enough to collect his share of earnings from contracted gigs, and went home, leaving Armstrong broke and in debt. Louis decided to stay to work his way out of the fix, signing English bandleader Jack Hylton as his manager.

Hylton arranged tours of Britain and the Continent, scheduling ample time between gigs and urging Armstrong to cut down on high-note trumpeting to rest his lips. Louis thrived under this management, and for a time considered making London his permanent base. Then Hylton got the idea of having the great American saxophonist Coleman Hawkins tour Europe with Armstrong as a team. Hawkins came over in March 1934, a tour was scheduled, and newspapers hailed the meeting of jazz giants. But just before the first concert, Louis backed out, leaving Hawkins to tour as a solo.

"I've figured it out and it seems it ain't going to do me any good," he explained lamely.[11] The real explanation was probably professional jealousy, fanned by his habitual insecurity. For months, he had been the center of attention, the American star whose arrival in Copenhagen drew ten thousand fans to the railroad station. Sharing the spotlight with another U.S. jazz star was just too painful.

Louis and Alpha stayed on in Europe to take a long vacation. They visited Ada Smith, the famous black American chanteuse and nightclub operator known as "Bricktop," at her home outside Paris. Louis signed up with a French booking agent and played a few gigs, but he and Alpha were spending a lot more money than he was earning. His new manager booked him

68   for a tour of France, Italy, and Switzerland. But his lip was in bad shape again, and Louis canceled the tour, provoking another legal wrangle.

When Louis and Alpha sailed for New York in January 1935, they had been away from home for a year and a half. A dozen years and a whole era in popular music would pass before Louis took his next trip abroad. Jazz was turning into swing, and the big bands would hold center stage during peace and war.

6

"GOOD EVENING, EVERYBODY!"

Louis was so short of money when he returned from Europe that he had to sell his thirty-two-hundred-dollar Buick for three hundred ninety dollars to cover his living expenses. And his prospects for the immediate future looked poor. The Depression still gripped the country, drastically reducing the number of cabarets, dance halls, and theaters that provided work for musicians. A court injunction obtained by Johnny Collins barred Armstrong from booking gigs through any other agent. He had not recorded in the United States for two years, and his Victor contract had not been renewed.

Lil was demanding a divorce and suing for money she claimed he owed her. Alpha was pressuring him for marriage. On top of everything else, his lips were in such bad shape that a doctor advised him to take six months off. As he had in the past when he needed a break from work, Louis went home to Chicago to rest.

He was clearly at a low point in his career. In fact, many jazz critics were saying that he was no longer

70   the great musician of the Hot Fives. They claimed he had abandoned "real" jazz in becoming a popular entertainer.

Real jazz, as critics defined it, was traditional black folk music played by small bands, with a great deal of free improvisation and interplay between the individual instruments. By turning away from this and performing with bands that simply provided backing for his trumpet and vocal solos, critics said Armstrong was betraying his art.

Jazz writer Rudi Blesh lamented "the loss to music which has resulted from Louis' devotion to swing."[1] John Hammond, among Louis's most enthusiastic supporters in the 1920s, said in 1939 that "Louis Armstrong's deterioration began when he chose to think of himself as a soloist, as a performer, rather than as an ensemble musician."[2]

There was some truth in the criticism. Louis's lip problems unquestionably hurt the quality of his playing on some gigs. He did play with some poor bands, occasionally sacrificed jazz feeling for high-register "circus" trumpeting, and he let himself be talked into using terrible material (a novelty number such as "Dusky Stevedore," which he recorded for Victor, is an example).

But even at his worst, Armstrong seldom gave a truly bad performance, and critical opinion of his best 1930s work has since changed. Looking back from the 1970s, critic Dan Morgenstern wrote: "Armstrong's mastery of his instrument and musical imagination continued to grow, far beyond the threshold of the thirties. What we [have] is jazz's greatest virtuoso and master improviser in the process of flowering and self-discovery."[3]

While Armstrong knew he was an artist, he did not take the idea of art as seriously as some people do. Impressing music critics was never as important to him as entertaining audiences and pouring out his feelings in his music. "I do not believe that any kind of art is sacred apart from what it truly expresses," he declared in *Swing That Music,* a ghostwritten book of his recollections and opinions which was published in 1936.[4]

Louis insisted he had not abandoned the music he loved—rather, the music had been drowned out by a flood of second-rate pop music that *called* itself jazz. The idea of free improvisation by the players was the core of jazz when it started back in New Orleans, but this basic idea got lost when jazz swept over the country, he or his ghost writer in *Swing That Music* noted.

Music publishing and record companies looking for "hit songs" wanted new jazz tunes written down and played the way they were written so the public could learn to sing them easily, Louis explained. The result was that jazz lost its originality and freshness and stopped growing. Most new jazz tunes were not really new but "the same old melodies and rhythms just twisted around . . . coarse beats or sticky-sweet phrases year after year." Good jazz musicians were now (in 1935) calling their music "swing," said Louis, "because they know how different it is from the stale brand of jazz they've got so sick of hearing."[5]

The first sign that swing was about to sweep the country came in the spring of 1935 when the Benny Goodman band arrived at Los Angeles's Palomar ballroom after a cross-country tour. The band featured swinging arrangements paced by Goodman's clarinet. For several months before the tour, it had been (playing) on a radio show called "Let's Dance," which was broadcast over a national network.

At first, the tour was a disaster: ticket sales were poor and dancers booed the hot numbers, forcing the band to play syrupy dance music which was not its strength. But when the depressed musicians got to the Palomar, they were amazed to be mobbed by thousands of cheering teenage fans. "Let's Dance" had

72   been broadcast too late in the evening to reach teenagers in the eastern part of the U.S. But Californians were well acquainted with the Goodman sound because of the time zone difference. They wanted more of it, and their passion for swing quickly spread east.

Like the Goodman band, most of the big bands which came to dominate the swing era were white. Black musicians were not yet working side by side with whites (though Goodman himself soon became the first white leader to hire black sidemen when he added Lionel Hampton to play vibes and Teddy Wilson on piano).

But most ballrooms and hotels were now open to black bands, and black bands like those of Duke Ellington, Count Basie, and Jimmie Lunceford could swing with anyone. Black entertainers also played a growing role in other branches of show business, including the movies. But they needed white agents to pave the way. Whites owned the theaters, movie companies, record companies, and ballrooms that provided the jobs, and most preferred not to deal with blacks as equals. Without white management, it was virtually impossible for a black, however talented, to rise in show business.[6]

Armstrong knew he needed a good agent, and he thought of Joe Glaser, manager of the Sunset Cafe when Louis gigged there a decade earlier. Glaser had opened a booking business in Chicago. He was just as tough, profane, and crude-mannered as Johnny Collins, had at least as many gangland connections, and had been in some sort of trouble with the law before Armstrong looked him up. But he was smarter than Collins, and he was genuinely fond of Louis.

No one knows exactly what sort of arrangement the two had. At first, it was based on nothing more than a handshake (though the musicians' union later in-

sisted on a formal agreement). Glaser booked the
gigs, hired and fired musicians, took care of taxes and
contracts and handled all the money, leaving
Armstrong free to concentrate on music. He would
take a large slice of Louis's earnings as his fee—
perhaps as much as fifty percent—but to Louis, he
was worth it. Louis trusted him completely and never
questioned his judgment or checked the books. In Joe
Glaser, he felt he had found the white ally Slippers had
advised him to look for when he left New Orleans
years before.

Many agents were unwilling to represent black entertainers, and Glaser saw an opportunity. Shortly after
taking on Armstrong, he met two band members in a
bar near the Apollo Theatre in New York. "I'm going to
buy you fellas a drink," he said. "It's my last five dollars,
but I'm going to tell you this. I'm going to control everything in black show business before I'm through." And
he almost did.[7]

He wasted no time getting Louis's career on track.
He arranged to buy out Johnny Collins, settled Louis's
financial problems with Lil, prepared a booklet of publicity material to send to newspapers, and began to
line up gigs for his client as soon as Louis's lip was
rested. Armstrong sang with Duke Ellington (another
Glaser client) at a Chicago one-nighter, and then em-
barked on a tour of the Midwest and South fronting a
band organized by Zilner Randolph.

Glaser went along, partly to make sure white club
owners didn't try to cheat the band in the South, where
it could be dangerous for black musicians to raise a
row. He shared the life of the bandsmen, except that
he, unlike the musicians, could always get a clean
room in a good hotel.

"It was tough traveling through the South in those
days," recalled Pops Foster, the bass player. "We had
two white guys with us—the bus driver and Joe Glaser.

74   If you had a colored bus driver back then, they'd lock him up in every little country town for 'speeding.' It was very rough finding a place to sleep. You couldn't get into hotels for whites, and the colored didn't have any hotels. You rented places in private homes, boarding houses and whorehouses. The food was awful, and we tried to find places where we could cook. We carried pots and pans around with us."[8]

Celebrity or not, Armstrong had to put up with the same treatment. "When I was coming along, a black man had hell," he told a magazine in 1967. "On the road he couldn't find no decent place to eat, sleep or use the toilet—service-station cats see a bus of colored bandsmen drive up and they would sprint to lock their rest room doors."[9]

After the tour, Armstrong went to New York to join the Luis Russell band, which was promptly renamed Louis Armstrong's Orchestra. Russell, a pianist, continued to manage the band and write most of the arrangements. But it was Armstrong who stood at center stage, and it was his trumpet and vocals that drew the fans. After a gig at Connie's Inn, the band drew capacity crowds with shows at the Lincoln Theatre in Philadelphia, the Apollo in Harlem, and the Paramount Theater in Times Square. For the next eight years, this would be Louis's regular band, a good swing band in its own right, though it was often playing accompaniment for what was essentially a one-man show.

Louis's natural shyness disappeared once the house lights went down and the curtain went up. He would step into the spotlight flashing his huge grin and spreading his arms wide; his customary greeting line, "Good evening, everybody!" always sounded warm and sincere because somehow, night after night, he truly felt that way.

Glaser was always urging him to "Smile, goddamit, smile!" or to "Make faces," but Louis hardly needed urging.[10] He loved to make people laugh, to feel the friendly response he could arouse in an audience and hear the excited applause rising as he built a trumpet solo toward its climax. His mugging no longer seemed crude or out of place. Now his facial contortions and eye rolling enhanced his singing, his comic patter, and his whole stage personality.

Armstrong was developing poise and stage presence worthy of Bojangles himself. Emceeing a show for the largely black audience at the Apollo one night, he had to introduce a white dance team whose name he could never remember. "He was announcing the various acts, and now it came time to announce the adagio," recalled a man who was there. "He said 'And now folks . . .' and you can see he's troubled and stalling and thinking what the hell are their names, 'cause he knew all the other acts personally. Finally he looks out in desperation and says, 'The two ofays!'"[11]

His showmanship made him a natural for Hollywood, and Armstrong became the first black musician to land a speaking role in the movies in 1936, when he appeared with Bing Crosby and the Jimmy Dorsey band in *Pennies From Heaven.* In 1937 he made *Artists and Models,* and in 1938 he appeared with Mae West in *Every Day's a Holiday.* In that same year, in the movie *Going Places,* Louis sang "Jeepers Creepers" to a horse—about the closest the Hollywood of the 1930s would come to letting a black sing a love song.[12]

Armstrong played some radio gigs in 1936, and by 1937 he was appearing regularly on shows with national sponsors such as Norge refrigerators and Fleischmann's yeast. While most big sponsors worried about associating blacks with their products for fear of offending white customers, some decided that Armstrong would win more goodwill for them than he would lose.

76   Glaser negotiated a recording contract for
Armstrong and the band with a company called
Decca. The contract would last for twelve years,
though it was interrupted by a two-year recording ban
imposed in 1942 by the musicians' union.

Decca pushed Armstrong even further in a commercial direction, often giving the band thin pop tunes
and comic novelties to record. Decca's policy of
teaming up its contract stars on the same record occasionally involved Louis in some ludicrous combinations,
as when he was paired with artists such as the Polyne-
sians and the Lyn Murray Chorus.

But the good outweighed the bad. Louis sang and
played on Decca records with such top singers as Billie
Holiday, Ella Fitzgerald, and Bing Crosby. He and the
band made memorable records of good popular
songs like "Thanks a Million," "You Are My Lucky Star,"
and "You Won't Be Satisfied Until You Break My Heart"
(the latter with wonderful vocal interplay between Louis
and Ella). And Armstrong began to make new records
of what he called his "good old good ones"[13]—tunes
like "Mahogany Hall Stomp," "Save It Pretty Mama,"
"West End Blues," "Monday Date," "Struttin' With Some
Barbecue," and "Sleepy Time Down South," which he
had first recorded as long as ten years before. Some
of these are superior to the original versions in the
opinion of many jazz fans. One reason was that the
Armstrong/Russell band was becoming a first-rate outfit
with the addition of fine jazzmen like trumpeter Henry
("Red") Allen, clarinetist Albert Nicholas, trombonist J.
C. Higginbotham, and a man many people rank as the
all-time best jazz drummer, Sidney ("Big Sid") Catlett.

In 1938, Louis and the band recorded the first jazz
version of a spiritual, "When the Saints Go Marching
In." The record was a hit, turning the old standby of
New Orleans funeral bands into a popular music stan-

dard that became an established part of Armstrong's repertoire.

In the same year, Louis finally divorced Lil and married Alpha Smith, who had been threatening a breach-of-promise suit. Glaser booked the band into the downtown Cotton Club in New York alongside the Bill Bojangles Robinson Revue, which pleased Louis because it gave him a chance to get to know his show business idol. It was there that he first saw Lucille Wilson, an attractive girl with a ready smile who danced in the chorus line of the revue, and who would become Louis's fourth wife.

Lucille was supporting her mother, two brothers, and a sister on a meager salary and sold cookies to the Cotton Club cast to raise extra money. One night, when she came to Armstrong's dressing room to drop off his box of cookies, Louis told her he would take all the boxes from then on. He took the cookies up to Harlem and gave them to schoolkids.

A few weeks later he recalled, "I just couldn't hold back the deep feeling and warmth I had for Lucille ever since I first laid eyes on her . . . swinging in that front line on the Cotton Club floor, looking beautifuller and beautifuller every night. I said, 'Lucille, I might as well tell you right now, I have eyes for you and have been having them for a long time. And if any of these cats in the show are shooting at you, I want to be in the running.'

"Lucille looked at me and just laughed. But before we both knew it, we were taking in the show [movies] between our shows. Riding uptown in Harlem every night after our last show. That's when I had that big long rust-colored Packard car that Mr. Glaser had bought for me, and boy was it sharp. It was the hottest car in town and the talk of the town. Bob Smiley, my right-hand man . . . used to drive this fine long Packard while Lucille and I would sit in the back seat."[14]

78   Armstrong had finally found what he called his "ideal girl," a woman of warmth, honesty, and intelligence. In October 1942, after he worked out a divorce settlement with Alpha, he and Lucille were married. It was a marriage that would last the rest of Louis's life and bring him a kind of happiness he had rarely known.

Unlike the others, Lucille accepted the fact that Louis's music came first. "That's why I married four times," Armstrong once explained. "The chicks didn't live with the horn. . . . That trumpet comes before everything—even before my wife Lucille. Had to be that way. I mean, I love her because she understands that. She's on my side."[15]

His chops, however, were continuing to be a problem. By 1940 his lips were scarred with tissue as hard as wood, and he could no longer play the rapidly rising and falling figures which had been such an important feature of his Hot Five work. He was also increasingly uncomfortable in the upper register. Louis's throat was also giving him trouble. He had a tonsillectomy in 1936, followed by an unsuccessful operation in 1937 to remove polyps near his vocal chords. The operations, plus the effects of smoking and nightly singing, left his voice rougher and more raspy than ever.

But his career was back in high gear by the end of the 1930s. His band had all the work it could get. He was doing regular radio shows, making an occasional movie, and his financial affairs were in excellent shape. He was an established star, talented and popular enough to rise above the most mediocre material.

In 1940, Louis played a role in a Broadway musical version of Shakespeare's *A Midsummer Night's Dream* called *Swinging the Dream* while doubling at the Cotton Club. In the musical, Louis appeared "dressed as a fireman and wearing a headpiece that suggests a skunk," according to a theater review.[16] He played only snatches of trumpet, and betrayed the fact that doubling at two gigs "was too much for his weary lip," according to *Down Beat* magazine. Nevertheless, the magazine concluded that "Louis walks away with honors,"[17] though the show flopped.

It was about this time that the swing craze was reaching its peak. Dozens of big bands were touring the nation to play hotel, theater, or roadhouse dates. The biggest names among them were overwhelmed with attention. Fans lined up for blocks to watch or dance to the music of Benny Goodman, Glenn Miller, Tommy Dorsey, Count Basie, or Artie Shaw. Their recordings broke all sales records and brought millions of nickels pouring into the nation's jukeboxes.

Somehow, Louis Armstrong's Orchestra was left behind in the rush. It wasn't that Louis and his band couldn't swing; as he himself said, swing was just a new variation on the kind of jazz he had always loved and played. But the most popular bands of the day were essentially dance bands, whose appeal lay in the distinctive styles of their arrangements and their "riffing" (repeating phrases played in unison by the brass or reed section). In contrast, Louis had become primarily a theatrical performer, and the show emphasized Louis's trumpet and vocal solos, with the rest of the band counting for little.

Besides, jazz fans were cheering for a whole new generation of trumpeters—players like Roy Eldridge, Harry James, Cootie Williams, and Dizzy Gillespie. All of these younger men owed something to Louis, and some had based their whole styles on his playing. But many of them were now technically superior to Armstrong. They could play higher and faster, and were less apt to fluff the occasional note.

Louis could still produce his marvelous mellow tone, and no one could surpass him in the ability to improvise variations on a melody. But too often, he didn't play up to his capacity. In the *Esquire* magazine polls of jazz fans that began in 1944, Armstrong was voted top jazz singer four times but was picked as the top trumpeter only twice.

Louis and the band continued to make coast-to-coast tours in the period 1941–43. Aside from a long stay at the Casa Manana in Los Angeles, most of the gigs were one-night stands. In 1944 a new band was formed to accompany him, with saxman Teddy McRae as musical director. The band starred in a jazz concert at New York's Metropolitan Opera House in early 1944 and went to New Orleans for a Jazz Foundation concert in early 1945. A brief revival of New Orleans music during the war years boosted Armstrong's popularity and also helped jazzmen like Kid Ory and Bunk Johnson make a temporary comeback from obscurity.

In 1943, Lucille purchased a modest house in Corona, Queens, a working-class neighborhood a few miles from Manhattan. Louis, who as usual was on the road at the time, had opposed the purchase, possibly because he feared the responsibility of "settling down." He had spent his life on the move, in trains and buses, hotel rooms, boardinghouses, and rented apartments.

Returning to New York, he telephoned Lucille before taking a taxi home and warned her he would go back to Manhattan if he didn't like what he saw. When his cab pulled up, he asked the driver to wait and rang the bell. Lucille opened the door.

"Welcome home, honey," she said.

"This is our home?"

"Yes."

He walked through the house from the basement to the attic. Lucille had fixed up every room and prepared a fine dinner. Louis loved the place. He invited the cabdriver to stay for dinner, and the three of them ate and drank for three or four hours.[18]

It was the first and last home Armstrong would ever **81**
own. He would become rich enough to live just about
anywhere in the world. But years later, when Lucille
tried to get him to buy a Long Island mansion with a
swimming pool, he wouldn't hear of it. The little house
on a quiet street in Queens, New York, was all he ever
wanted.

7

THE AMBASSADOR OF JAZZ

During the Second World War, Louis Armstrong's Orchestra and its leader were in steady demand. They played at service bases all over the United States and broadcast regularly over the Armed Forces Radio Service.

By the end of the war, however, America's musical tastes were undergoing major changes, and some of them threatened to undermine Armstrong's career. He had never won a big following among young white swing fans before the war. And his chances to do it vanished when public enthusiasm for big band swing cooled off with astonishing speed.

Within a year and a half of VJ Day in September 1945, the big bands, which had dominated popular music for ten years, were out of business. The club owners who hired the bands could no longer afford them, partly because musicians' pay had risen to high levels during the war when the government was hiring them to entertain servicemen. On top of that, young fans were shifting their allegiance from dance bands to

84 vocalists. Singers such as Frank Sinatra, Perry Como, Nat ("King") Cole, Billy Eckstine, Peggy Lee, and Billie Holiday—most of whom had made their reputations singing with big bands—were now the stars. They were touring as soloists, often with only a piano accompanist, and recording with studio bands assembled just to back them up.

A few big bands like Ellington, Goodman, Basie, Woody Herman, Stan Kenton, and the Glenn Miller band (reassembled under other leaders after Miller's death in the war) managed to carry on. But most of them broke up for lack of bookings.

Louis was also losing his audience among young black jazz fans, who had idolized him in his early days. They were turning to "rhythm and blues," a commercial variety of the blues with a heavy beat and often sexually explicit lyrics, which helped lay the groundwork for rock and roll. And then there was bebop. Pioneered by jazzmen like saxman Charlie Parker and trumpeter Dizzy Gillespie, bebop featured fractured rhythms, weird chording, and wild solo swoops that often seemed to lose track of the melody.

Many young jazz musicians embraced bebop enthusiastically, but Louis hated it. "Some of that fantastic stuff, when they tear out from the first note and you ask yourself 'What the hell's he playing?'—that's not for me," he said. "Personally, I wouldn't play that kind of horn if I played a hundred years."[1]

There was also a revival of Dixieland in the 1940s, the New Orleans–style small-band jazz popularized by white musicians in the 1920s. It inspired Hollywood to film a jazz musical called New Orleans in 1946, with a cast that included Billie Holiday, the big band of Woody Herman, and a small band of New Orleans musicians headed by Armstrong. There were speaking and singing roles in the picture for both Louis and Billie Holiday. The plot and dialogue re-

flected the ludicrous clichés and vaguely racist ideas
which typified Hollywood's treatment of jazz subjects
at the time. In one scene, Holiday, playing a house-
maid, introduced the song "You Don't Know What It
Means to Miss New Orleans," explaining to her white
mistress that she had made it up while dusting.[2]

Watching rehearsals for the movie in a California
studio, jazz promoter Leonard Feather got the idea of
organizing a concert at New York's Carnegie Hall that
would showcase Armstrong with a small band. When
Louis (and Joe Glaser) insisted that his big band be included, a compromise was made: Armstrong would
do the first half of the show with clarinetist Edmond
Hall's sextet and play the second half with his own big
band. Billie Holiday would sing songs from *New
Orleans* to publicize the upcoming movie.

The concert, in February 1947, gave Louis's New
York fans their first chance since the 1930s to hear him
play a straight jazz performance. Its success led to another even more successful concert at Town Hall that
May. The backup band assembled for this gig included
Teagarden on trombone, trumpeter Bobby Hackett,
clarinetist Peanuts Hucko, Sid Catlett from the big band
on drums, Dick Carey on piano, and Bob Haggart on
bass, all of them distinguished jazzmen. No one suggested including the big band. The highlight of the concert was a memorable vocal duet between Louis and
Teagarden on "Rockin' Chair," which audiences would
shout for in years to come whenever the two musicians
shared a stage.

Joe Glaser had always preferred to put Louis in a
big, splashy stage setting surrounded by lots of musicians. But the sensation created by the Town Hall concert convinced him that small-band jazz was back and
that his client's future lay here. Louis Armstrong's Orchestra was disbanded after finishing up a theater gig

in Philadelphia that summer, and Louis never toured with a big band again.

In the meantime, Glaser was working to set up a small band of star musicians on a permanent basis to accompany Armstrong on tour. The collapse of the big bands had left many top jazzmen temporarily out of work, which made Glaser's job easier. The group he assembled was even better than the band for the Town Hall concert: the incomparable Earl Hines and Dick Carey alternating on piano; trombonist Teagarden; New Orleanian Barney Bigard, "the best clarinetist ever," in Louis's opinion; Catlett and Cozy Cole alternating on drums; bassist Morty Korb; and Bobby Hackett as music director.

Glaser booked the first gig for Louis Armstrong and his All Stars at a Los Angeles nightclub. Opening night in August 1947 drew an audience of celebrities including every big-name musician in town. The club continued to fill its tables every night, and the group's stay was extended.

Within two years, the All Stars had become "the highest paid unit of its size in existence," according to *Down Beat*. They would continue to play and draw crowds for another twenty years, though the personnel gradually changed as band members moved on to other gigs. Joe Sullivan replaced Hines and Trummy Young replaced Teagarden in 1951. Bigard was replaced in 1955 by Edmond Hall, though Barney later returned for another All Stars year.

The female vocalist for nearly fifteen years was Velma Middleton, brought from the big band. Middleton resembled a circus fat lady and was not a very talented singer. But she worked well with Louis in humorous duets and onstage clowning (she would occasionally finish a song on the floor after a spectacular split). Her longtime stay with the band suggests that showmanship played a big part in the All Stars' success. In fact, Armstrong's own showmanship was probably more important than all the jazz talent in the band in assuring the capacity crowds for most All Star gigs.

The All Stars spent most of the time on the road doing a series of one-night gigs and were constantly hopping on and off trains, buses, or planes. Joe Glaser was pushing them hard, and many of them felt overworked. But Armstrong seemed to relish the work, the late hours, and even the traveling. "I never felt yet that I didn't want to get on that stand," he told a reporter."[3]

Louis had always had a remarkable ability to catch up on lost sleep whenever he got the chance; he could sit down and fall asleep at a moment's notice, and wake up just as quickly. He took special care of the parts of his body he considered to be most important, relying on Swiss Kriss for his stomach and treating his lips before every performance with a special salve made for him in Germany. His valet, Doc Pugh, would open a leather case containing the salve, bottles of a medicinal solution, and sterile applicators. Pugh would apply the ointments with special attention to the calloused center part of Louis's upper lip, which bore the brunt of mouthpiece pressure.[4]

By this point in his career, his lips were as tough as shoe leather. But they could still get very sore and sometimes made trumpeting so painful he could barely play. According to All Stars drummer Cozy Cole, Armstrong "really played" about eighty percent of the time; his chops were down the other twenty.[5]

Despite the wearing pace, the All Stars were a happy group. The music was good, the money was good, and the association with Armstrong made many bandsmen famous, exposing their talents to bigger audiences than they could have ever reached on their own.

88   Louis made sure that all of them got a chance to shine as featured soloists. An All Stars show would open with Louis's trumpet leading the group through a fast Dixieland standard like "Muskrat Ramble" followed by a slow number associated with Armstrong, such as "Memories of You" or "Solitude." Then, each band member would be featured on one or more numbers where Louis played almost nothing at all. The band's total repertoire was fairly limited, though Louis tried to include something new and fresh in each show.

The show usually concluded with Louis playing and singing some of his current hits. In 1949 he recorded a currently popular song called "That Lucky Old Sun" for Decca, accompanied by a big band and a choir. For the flip side, Armstrong himself chose a ballad called "Blueberry Hill," which he remembered hearing in the early forties. His gravelly vocal made "Blueberry Hill" one of the big hits of the year and gave Decca the idea that Armstrong might have "Top 40" potential. The company began to use him to "cover" hits recorded by other singers, a standard practice in the record business. If Perry Como or Frankie Laine scored big with a song, for example, Decca would have Louis record the same tune—figuring that it was a proven winner and that Louis's version was bound to be different.[6]

In the next few years, Louis's voice became familiar to millions of teenage record buyers on records like "La Vie En Rose," "C'est Si Bon," "A Kiss to Build a Dream On," "I Get Ideas," "Ramona" and "I'll Walk Alone." These were commercial recordings with little jazz quality; in fact, many critics complained that the All Stars were playing too many show tunes and popular ballads and not enough of the kind of jazz that made Armstrong's reputation in the 1920s. Louis's response was "There's no such thing as a bad song"—an exaggerated way of saying that any song had good things in it that good musicians could bring out. His own musicianship and the personality he projected in his voice **89** turned ordinary songs into hits and permanently stamped those songs as his own.

In fact, when *Time* magazine did a cover story on Armstrong in 1949, many readers were amazed to learn that the man they knew as a jovial singer of pop tunes was a jazz immortal; some were not even aware that he played the trumpet. His fame had obscured his real importance.

Armstrong's international reputation was revitalized in 1948 when the All Stars appeared at the International Jazz Festival in Nice, France, the first major jazz event of the postwar era in Europe. People came from all over Europe to attend, many of them traveling by bicycle because cars and gasoline were still scarce on the war-shattered Continent. Eighteen radio stations broadcast the festival concerts from day to day.

Armstrong showed European fans that his talents as a trumpeter had not disappeared since his last visit in the 1930s. "I was particularly struck by the almost puritanical simplicity of his playing," gushed British critic Humphrey Lyttelton. "All the old trappings and ornaments . . . of his earlier phases have been swept away . . . and there was left a music which, with its purity and serenity, brought us perhaps nearer to the fountain-head of his genius than we have ever been before."[7] The president of France presented a beautiful Sèvres vase to Louis, the "King of Jazz."

In 1949 the All Stars began a continuing series of overseas appearances that earned Louis recognition as an ambassador of goodwill of great value to his country. When the band arrived in Stockholm, Sweden, a local paper printed an eight-page special jazz section in his honor. In Rome he was met by the Roman New Orleans Jazz Band and taken home by the leader to a spaghetti dinner prepared by the leader's mother, a countess.[8] Louis and Lucille also had an audience with Pope Pius XII, whom Louis described in later years as "a little bitty feller I liked so well, the first [pope] I met." When the pope asked the Armstrongs whether they had any children, Louis replied, "Not yet, but we're having a lot of fun trying."

The band toured Europe in 1952, Australia and Japan in 1954, Europe again in 1955, Australia and the Far East for a second time in 1956, and Britain later the same year. There was a major tour of South America in 1957, and another long European trip in 1959. "Man, with all that thinking and studying about what's going to come next, I'd end up saying 'Pleased to meet you' in German when I got off the plane in Italy," Louis recalled. "But when I say 'Good Evening, Everybody,' they know I *mean* it—same with music, just do what come natural."[9]

When his lips were healthy and he was not straining for high-register effects, Armstrong's horn playing did indeed seem to flow naturally from the same inner wellsprings as his personality. A musician who asked Louis what he thought about when he was improvising got this advice: "Just close your eyes and remember the good times you had when you were a kid. Then you'll find the music will come out." Armstrong told a journalist who asked the same question: "I just think about all my happy days and memories and the notes come out, always has been that way. To me, jazz has got to be a happy music, you've got to love it to play."[10]

His fierce competitiveness was another force that could bring out his musical best. On a 1953 U.S. tour by Armstrong and Benny Goodman, says Bobby Hackett, Goodman insisted that it was his package and Louis would have to follow his orders. "You're nothin'," said Armstrong in a cold rage—and made his point by outplaying the King of Swing so badly that Goodman became ill. "Pops came close to killing him without touching him, just playing," said Hackett.[11]

In all his travels, it was his visits to Africa that meant **91** the most to him. "My ancestors came from here," he said in expressing his pleasure to be in Ghana in 1956, where his rendition of "Black and Blue" brought tears to the eyes of President Kwame Nkrumah.[12] The first concert drew a crowd of a hundred thousand Ghanaians, many of whom had probably never heard of Armstrong. But Louis quickly won them over. He and Lucille danced with tribal chieftains, and Louis visited local schools to demonstrate his trumpet to pupils. He had always taken pride in being what he called a "pure-blooded" black from this part of Africa (once known as the Gold Coast), and he was delighted when he managed to find reminders of his family there.[13]

But Armstrong was getting a chillier reception from African-American fans back home, where the civil rights movement was beginning to gather momentum in the late 1950s.

His overall popularity had never been higher, boosted by the huge success of his 1955 recording of "Mack the Knife," a song from the musical *The Threepenny Opera*, then running on Broadway. A poll ranked Armstrong with Charlie Chaplin as the all-time most famous American worldwide.

But many black Americans blamed Armstrong for not using his fame to speak out against the treatment of blacks in United States society. They felt his respectful manner, his grinning and mugging before his predominantly white (and sometimes segregated) audiences tended to endorse the status quo. They recalled his successes singing "coon songs" like "Snowball" and "Shine," which seemed to demean blacks. His theme song, "Sleepy Time Down South," written in 1931, was a nostalgic hymn of the pre–Civil War South, which Armstrong refused to change except to substitute the word "folks" for "darkies." When he agreed to play the role of King of the Zulus in the 1949 Mardi Gras, a

92 segregated spectacle which was the very symbol of blacks' second-class citizenship, some blacks publicly condemned him as an "Uncle Tom."

And some white jazz lovers felt the same way. "It is hard to understand why [he] behaves when he appears in person like a blackface minstrel," wrote jazz critic Whitney Balliett in the early 1950s. "He must be weary, and perhaps this sort of posing is a prop, or perhaps he doesn't even realize he is doing it anymore."[14]

Even Armstrong's kind of music reinforced his old fogy, Uncle Tom image among young black musicians in the vanguard of postwar jazz. The bebop and "progressive" jazz of the 1950s seemed to carry a message of political militancy as well as artistic change. Instrumentalists soared and dipped to the limits of the musical scale, wrenching new sounds from their instruments, leaving melody far behind (or ignoring it) in flights of technical brilliance. It didn't matter that many listeners could not follow. Some prominent jazz soloists emphasized that point by turning their backs on the audience while they explored chord sequences. They also turned their backs on traditional jazz, which—to many blacks, at least—symbolized the old, dead South of repressed Negroes and white supremacy. Cool and inaccessible, their music seemed to suit the mood of hostility and protest that was building in black society.

For Louis, the accusations of Tomming were doubly painful because he could hardly defend himself. All his life he had loved to entertain people and had never put on airs with his fans. He never gave a concert without signing autographs for anyone who asked. What some people took for servility was actually simple good manners. Respectful behavior to strangers was rooted in his upbringing, and he could no more abandon it than he could make his smile less dazzling.

It was not that Armstrong was ignorant of prejudice nor unscarred by it. His New Orleans boyhood and years of touring the South gave him a keen awareness of these attitudes. But he was raised to respect people until they showed themselves unworthy of respect. It is to his credit that such experiences did not leave him with bitter feelings toward the white race in general.

It was typical of Louis that he could ignore the contradictions in "coon songs," says jazz critic James Collier. "They were only a modest part of his repertory, and he could have dispensed with them. But he seems to have *liked* to sing them. It was a way of ingratiating himself with whites, who increasingly . . . became his major audience. . . . A lot of his appeal for so diverse an audience had to do with this willingness to be friendly, ingratiating or, as was so often said, 'humble.'"[15]

Criticism of Armstrong's stage manner, his joking and toothy grimacing, made no allowance for the fact that he was the product of an era when black entertainers conformed to the vaudeville image. Billie Holiday, another black jazz star who knew plenty about race prejudice, summed it up best after watching an Armstrong television performance. "I love Pops," she said. "He 'Toms' from the heart."[16]

No one who knew Louis took the Uncle Tom accusations seriously. And the truth is that Louis did as much as anyone to change the attitudes that kept blacks from getting a full share of the American dream. His musical genius and loving personality made whites reconsider racist ideas they had taken for granted. As early as 1929, he recorded "Black and Blue" with a lyric that undoubtedly pricked the conscience of many white listeners: "I'm white inside/ but that don't help my case/ 'cause I can't hide/ what is in my face."

Armstrong did not make a point of publicly protesting racial injustice, but he was not afraid to speak out when he felt it was called for. In the fall of 1957 he was on tour in Grand Forks, North Dakota, during the Little Rock school crisis, and watched on his dressing room TV as a mob of whites jeered and cursed at the few black students trying to enter Little Rock's Central High School. A reporter from the Grand Forks paper came backstage after the show to interview the visiting celebrity and got more than he bargained for. Armstrong said that President Eisenhower had demonstrated "no guts" in failing to enforce federal school integration laws. "The way they are treating my people in the South, the government can go to hell," Louis declared. When the paper put the quotes on the news wire, "the verbal blast echoed virtually around the world," said *Down Beat* magazine.[17]

Armstrong's outburst, which resulted in several concert cancellations in the South, may have had something to do with the president's decision a few days later to integrate Little Rock schools with federal troops. But it did not help Louis's standing with the administration. When the All Stars played Washington before their South American tour later that year, aides arranged to have Louis invited to the White House for lunch, assuming the president would dine with the "jazz ambassador." But Eisenhower never appeared. He sent his chief of staff, who shook Louis's hand and walked away.[18]

When Louis was touring the world in the 1950s, he had no official government sponsorship, even though it was clear that his music and especially his personality were winning a lot of goodwill for the nation. *The New York Times* wrote in 1956 that "America's secret weapon is a blue note in a minor key, and Louis Armstrong is its most effective ambassador."[19] Broadcaster Edward R. Murrow began to film portions of All Star tours. The film footage was edited to produce a TV show and later made part of a movie about

Armstrong's career (*Satchmo the Great*) in which Louis **95** played himself.

But the State Department paid little attention until 1957, when communists were eagerly calling the world's attention to the protest marches and other signs of racial tension in America. The State Department offered to sponsor an Armstrong tour of the Soviet Union and Eastern Europe, hoping his personality and prestige would help counter propagandists' image of the United States as a racist society.

Louis was planning to make the tour at the time of the Little Rock incident, but his anger over Little Rock impelled him to pull out. "People over there will ask me what's wrong with my country," he explained. "What am I supposed to say?"[20] His refusal, like his blast at Eisenhower, made him enemies, though it hardly affected his career. The chance to go to the Soviet Union never came again, and this was one of the few places in the world he never visited.

In 1960 the U.S. government did begin sponsoring Armstrong's foreign tours, starting with an African trip, for which a soft-drink company helped underwrite the costs. Joe Glaser lined up enough gigs to ensure that the tour would also be financially profitable. The trip began with the All Stars' second visit to Ghana and continued for forty-five concerts in a total of eleven countries in both West and East Africa. Glaser had tried to schedule gigs in South Africa, but the South African government banned a visit by the racially mixed All Stars under its apartheid laws.

In Ibadan, Nigeria, the All Stars filled all fifty thousand seats for two concerts in an open-air arena in the rain. In the new Republic of the Congo (now Zaire), where a bitter struggle between political factions was under way, the people forgot their differences in the excitement over the All Stars' visit and cheered wildly when Armstrong drove past behind a truckload of na-

96   tive dancers. An African song was composed in his
honor. "They call you Satchmo, but to us you are
Okuka Lokole," the lyric went. Okuka, Louis learned,
was a jungle wizard who charmed wild beasts with
music.[21]

"When one observes the reaction of audiences
and the general public, it is brought home with force
what a wonderful ambassador Louis is for his country,"
wrote a resident of Nairobi, Kenya, after the All Stars'
visit. "There is a fair amount of anti-American feeling in
Kenya. . . . Armstrong, more than any other visiting
American, has helped to overcome prejudice and
made friendship. . . ."[22]

The State Department made it official. It issued a
statement saying that Louis Armstrong had become one
of America's best ambassadors "through the magic Es-
peranto of his music."[23]

8

"MY WHOLE LIFE IS TO BLOOOOW THAT HORN!"

During his world tours with the All Stars, Armstrong was best known for his huge smile, the warmth of his personality, and the unmistakable sound of his singing voice. Years of performing in smoke-filled clubs and his own heavy cigarette smoking had left him with chronic bronchitis, which was partly responsible for his raspy sound. He also suffered from growths on his vocal cords, which he may have had since childhood. Two operations in the 1930s had failed to correct the condition, and Louis finally accepted the fact that he was never going to sound like a romantic crooner. It turned out to be a big boost for his career, of course. There were a lot of romantic crooners around, but only one singer like Satchmo.

Yet Armstrong thought of himself as a trumpet player first and foremost. And despite his lip problems, he did some of his finest trumpeting in his fifties, an age when horn players generally begin to slip a little. He was at his best as an instrumentalist at recording sessions, where the emphasis was strictly on the music,

98   rather than at live performances where showmanship was a big concern.

In 1954 the All Stars recorded an album called *Louis Armstrong Plays W. C. Handy* on which Armstrong's brilliant trumpeting surprised even his most loyal fans. The album became a jazz classic, which renewed interest in lesser-known compositions by Handy, the composer of "St. Louis Blues." The group followed with another album called *Satch Plays Fats,* in which Armstrong outdid some of his 1930s recordings of Fats Waller numbers like "Ain't Misbehavin'" and "Blue Turning Gray Over You."[1]

In late 1956 and early 1957, producer Milt Gabler assembled the All Stars to record a set of four albums for Decca called Satchmo: A Musical Autobiography of Louis Armstrong. Gabler's idea was to record Armstrong and the All Stars replaying the most memorable records of Louis's peak years, trying to reconstruct the arrangements and even the recording conditions (although the recording equipment would be far superior, of course). The "autobiography" included forty-two numbers ranging from Louis's first records with King Oliver through the Hot Fives to his big-band work in the 1930s. There are a few weak spots in the series, but the general quality of the jazz is excellent— and on some tunes, Armstrong plays better horn than he did on the originals.

The album *King of the Zulus,* one of the Decca set, was "superb" to critic Whitney Balliett, who greeted the album set enthusiastically after years of complaining that Armstrong was sacrificing jazz artistry for show business effects. "Playing in a legato, low-toned way, he constructs a series of seemingly lazy, halting phrases that rival anything he has recorded," Balliett said. "His voice, which has put on a lot of weight over the years, is well controlled and wholly free of vaudeville effects."[2]

While the years were taking a toll on his lips, lungs, **99** and vocal chords, Armstrong's musical imagination was undiminished. He was inspired by melody ("You got to play the melody," King Oliver had said) and never wandered far from it in playing or singing a song. But the way he phrased a melody added something new and distinctive. Armstrong published only a few songs of his own. Yet he qualifies as an important jazz composer on the basis of the hundreds of melodic phrases he invented but never wrote down. Some were carefully worked out over an extended period of time, but he improvised most on the spur of the moment while playing trumpet onstage or in recording studios.

Many of the young musicians who were taking jazz in new directions in the 1950s and 1960s, the creators of bebop and the "free form" jazz which followed, continued to regard Armstrong as a relic of the past. They laughed when Louis expressed admiration for the Guy Lombardo band, whose sweet dance music was the symbol of everything hip jazz lovers found square and unhip. What Louis liked about Lombardo was that the band played tunes well and danceably, with great attention to the melody.

You couldn't dance to bebop, and it was hard to even follow the tune. It was not surprising that bop never won a large following among record buyers. When rock and roll swept the music business beginning in the mid-1950s, bebop and all other jazz styles lost popularity, particularly among younger people, leaving many jazz musicians out of work. Yet Armstrong's audience appeal just kept growing.

Armstrong was not stuck in the past. He respected the talent of many modern musicians, including at least one famous rock band. When he was on the road well into his sixties, he traveled with a portable record player and about twenty long-playing records, mostly of his own music. "Whenever I want to reach back for

100 one of them fine old tunes I got them here to refresh my memory," he said. "But I've also got Barbra Streisand—she can sing awhile, can't she?—and the Beatles. It's music, and they swing."[3]

Touring Europe in the summer of 1959, Armstrong and the All Stars arrived in Spoleto, Italy, to play at a music festival organized by composer Gian-Carlo Menotti. They were accompanied by Dr. Alexander Schiff, because Lucille worried about the dangers of sudden illness for Louis and other bandsmen in countries where they didn't speak the language and where medical care might not be up to U.S. standards. She asked Joe Glaser to find a doctor, and Glaser persuaded his friend Dr. Schiff to join the All Stars on tour.

At the chilly castle in Spoleto where the group was staying, Dr. Schiff was awakened one night by Armstrong's valet, who told him Louis was sick. Schiff found him on his knees, holding on to his bed, his ankles swollen and his lungs filled with fluid. Suspecting a respiratory infection, the doctor had him rushed to a hospital. He arranged for a nurse who could speak English and noted on Armstrong's chart that Louis was allergic to penicillin (because of this, Schiff always carried other antibiotics).

The following night, informed that Armstrong was running a hundred-and-four-degree temperature, the doctor dressed hastily and raced to Armstrong's hospital room to find an intern filling a syringe with penicillin. He snatched it away and dashed it to the floor, possibly saving his patient's life.[4]

Louis had suffered a major heart attack, though Dr. Schiff at first denied this to news reporters who besieged the hospital, telling them it was pneumonia. Joe Glaser may have feared the truth would hurt future bookings, since club owners might not welcome a performer who could drop dead in mid-performance. In any case, Armstrong seemed to recover quickly and

insisted on leaving the hospital within a week. He went **101**
to Rome and spent a whole night drinking and singing,
and then flew to New York, where he put in a token
appearance at a jazz concert, playing trumpet for fifteen minutes to wild applause. All this was the height of
foolishness for a seriously ill man, but Louis simply refused to accept his condition.

Over the years, he had suffered from ulcers, dia-
betes, chronic bronchitis, and varicose veins—
perhaps inevitable after a lifetime of sitting in cramped
buses, eating poorly and irregularly, dosing himself
with Swiss Kriss, drinking and smoking too much, and
performing on his feet until the late hours. Until then, he
had somehow been able to rise above his physical
problems, but the heart attack changed things.

It robbed him of the strength essential to his art.
While he remained in relatively good health, and
made some attempts to change his diet as doctors advised, he never again approached his top form as a
trumpeter. By the mid-1960s he was suffering from a
chronic heart condition which left him so short of breath
he could often do little more than go through the mo-
tions in his horn solos. He also had to change his singing style, sticking to short phrases that allowed him to
catch a quick breath in between.[5]

But there were still moments when he would somehow rise to his old standards, and some were cap-
tured on record. In 1960, sitting in with a group of
young musicians called the Dukes of Dixieland,
Armstrong played trumpet as though the years had
fallen away. The band seemed to inspire Louis and
Louis obviously inspired the band; records like "Avalon"
and "Limehouse Blues" are among the best the Dukes
ever made.

After the Dukes came the Duke. In 1961, Duke
Ellington sat in as guest pianist with the All Stars for a
famous recording session that produced seventeen

records in two days. It was the first time that Armstrong and Ellington—perhaps the two most important figures in jazz history—had recorded together. Even though Louis had just returned from a hard road trip and his battered lips were feeling unusually sore, his trumpet soared on numbers like "The Beautiful American," and the musicianship of the two great jazzmen lifted the whole series above the ordinary.

These records became part of jazz legend. But the record that scored highest with the public and gave Louis one of the biggest thrills of his life was a song he recorded in December 1963. A new musical called *Hello Dolly* was about to open on Broadway, and the producers wanted someone to record the title song to help promote the show. They arranged with Glaser to have the song recorded by Armstrong accompanied by the All Stars and a string section.

"Hello Dolly" was an undistinguished tune, hardly good enough to stand on its own outside of the show. Armstrong reportedly shook his head in dismay when he first read the sheet music at the start of the recording session.[6] But something good happened when the All Stars lit into it, beginning with an eight-bar banjo introduction and the happy sound of Louis's voice. His swinging vocal and strong trumpet chorus, ably backed by the band, transformed the routine pop tune and brought a huge response from record buyers. "Hello Dolly" edged onto *Billboard* magazine's charts of hit records in February 1964, and by May it pushed past a Beatles number to become the top single in the country.

With rock totally dominating the record business, jazz fans were delighted to see one of their own score a rare popular triumph. That summer, when the All Stars played a one-night stand at the Metropole in New York's Times Square, musicians threw a party for Louis at a bar across the street. Banners reading "You Beat

The Beatles!" were hung on the walls; guests including **103** Duke Ellington, Lionel Hampton, Ben Webster, Eddie Condon, and other top jazzmen played a few riffs and raised glasses in a toast to "Pops."

"Hello Dolly" was on the charts for twenty-two weeks overall. The producer reassembled the band to record enough old Armstrong standards to make up an album with the new hit, and the album also went to the top of the charts.

The success of "Hello Dolly" gave a major boost to Armstrong's career. Hollywood pursued him with more movie parts, and he was invited to appear on one TV show after another, from the Ed Sullivan show to "What's My Line" (where he sang a chorus of "Hello Dolly" without accompaniment). Audiences at All Stars concerts insisted on the song, and Louis began making it a regular feature.

In 1969 he appeared in the movie version of *Hello Dolly*, starring Barbra Streisand. He was on camera for only two and a half minutes in his thirty-sixth (and last) movie role, but his playing and singing stole the show and helped turn the film into a box office smash. It was not unusual for audiences to applaud only at the moment near the end when the camera zooms in for a close-up of Louis's face.[7]

During all these years, Armstrong continued to travel almost without letup. All Stars tours between 1961 and 1967 took him to Africa, Australia, New Zealand, Mexico, Iceland, India, Singapore, and Eastern and Western Europe. He also played gigs from coast to coast in the United States, including one-nighters, in spite of his friends' advice to slow down. "Those one-nighters aren't so bad," he told a writer in the 1950s. "I can make it in New York without trouble. But I don't mind traveling, and that's where the audiences are, in the towns and cities. I want to hear that applause. . . ."[8] In the 1960s, suffering from ulcers

104 and kidney disease as well as heart problems, there were many times when he was so exhausted that he wanted to stop. But he kept pushing himself, feeling he had to keep his name before the public, and often quoted an old adage: "In show business, you've got to die to prove that you're sick."[9]

In 1965 he accepted a concert gig in New Orleans, his first visit to his hometown in twelve years. He had vowed many years before not to perform there until city fathers scrapped the racial laws that forbade blacks and whites to play on the same bandstand. "I ain't going back and let them white folks in my own hometown be whipping on my head and killing me for my hustle," he told a reporter. "I don't care if I never see New Orleans again."[10] When the laws finally were changed and Louis did come home, he was presented with a key to the city.

He was back on the pop charts in 1968 with "What A Wonderful World," which remains one of his most frequently played records. But a great deal of the material he was asked to record as a singer in the late 1960s was mediocre and downright unsuitable. One album featured Armstrong interpretations of country and western songs. At another recording session he was asked to sing "His Father Wore Long Hair"—a treacly song in waltz time that had something to do with Jesus's father—accompanied by a chorus of celebrities. This was followed by "We Shall Overcome" and "Give Peace a Chance." The best thing about the latter record is Louis's joking aside, "Give me a little ol' peace, deah", which suggests he didn't take the number very seriously.[11]

The album *Disney Songs The Satchmo Way*, recorded in 1968, features Louis singing and playing songs from Walt Disney movies. While the album is aimed at children and most of the songs (like "Whistle While You Work" and "The Ballad of Davy Crockett") are childish and trite, Louis's performance lifts everything to a higher level. The trumpet choruses are perhaps the most remarkable solos he ever recorded, considering his age and the state of his health.

Dr. Schiff referred him to a New York heart specialist in the fall of 1968, when Louis was gasping for breath and his body was accumulating fluid. The specialist, Dr. Gary Zucker, told him he was suffering from heart failure and should go into the hospital immediately. But Louis refused and "practically ran out of my office," Dr. Zucker reported.

Louis spent the next two weeks in Harlem, where he "sort of had a time on the town," as he put it—drinking, gambling, and socializing with the black jazz fans to whom he had always been a hero.[12] This return to old haunts seems to have been his way of denying the idea of his own mortality. After two weeks, his body was so swollen with fluid that he could not get his shoes on. A thoroughly frightened Armstrong finally put himself in the hospital, where doctors stabilized his condition with drugs.

He was back in the hospital the following February, when an emergency tracheotomy had to be performed to clear up congestion in his lungs. While Louis was recovering, Joe Glaser was brought to another room in the same hospital after suffering a stroke. Louis went to visit him when he heard about it, but found him in a coma. Glaser died on June 4 without regaining consciousness.

The death of the manager to whom he had entrusted his career for more than thirty years shook Louis badly. But it did not keep him from resuming his career as soon as he could. He was back on the road playing gigs that summer.

When he wasn't performing, he was at his desk writing, as though he were trying to get things on paper while there was still time. He had already left a

106 larger written record than any jazz musician in history, including more than two dozen magazine pieces and two books (*Swing That Music* in 1936 and *Satchmo: My Life in New Orleans,* his memoir of his early days, which was published in 1954). He also wrote hundreds of letters. Louis was an enthusiastic correspondent with a good ear for language, and spent a great deal of time at the typewriter he carried on road trips, pecking out single-spaced letters to friends or fans.

The 1954 book was supposed to be the first part of a two-part autobiography, and Louis worked on the sequel for many years. This manuscript has been lost, although other autobiographical writings from the period 1954 to 1971 have survived. One of these manuscripts, written in longhand and covering a hundred twenty-nine pages, includes a long memoir titled "Negroe [sic] Neighborhood" which bitterly criticizes New Orleans blacks for failing to stick together to improve their lives. Another manuscript, written after his second hospital stay, is more typically Armstrong. It is an "open letter" which tells, among other things, of Louis's admiration for Bill Robinson and recounts how he sold his hospital nurses on the benefits of Swiss Kriss.[13]

On July 3, 1970, Louis was the guest of honor at a huge party and concert in Hollywood's Shrine Auditorium. Some sixty-seven hundred people, many of them from show business, turned out to honor him on the night before what was assumed to be his seventieth birthday. He was presented with a twelve-foot birthday cake and a white wicker rocking chair. Hoagy Carmichael emceed the show, and Louis himself sang "Sleepy Time," "Blueberry Hill," and "Hello Dolly," clowning and mugging happily even though his kidney ailment was giving him considerable pain. A week later, he was at the Newport Jazz Festival in Rhode Island, where a "Salute to Satch" night was scheduled. A downpour started just as he went onstage, soaking the **107** audience, which was sitting and standing in an open field. But the crowd refused to leave. They stayed cheering in the rain while Louis, on the covered stage, ran through a medley of his hits as quickly as he could to spare his listeners unnecessary exposure.

Louis resumed a full working schedule in September, playing an All Stars gig in Las Vegas. He went to London in October to play and sing at a charity concert and was back in Las Vegas with the All Stars in December. He made frequent appearances on TV, including a talk show date in February 1971 in which he sang duets with Bing Crosby.

In March of that year, the Glaser office booked the All Stars for a two-week engagement at the Empire Room of New York's Waldorf Astoria hotel. Louis was in such poor health that Dr. Zucker wanted him to cancel the date and go into the hospital. "You could drop dead while you're performing," the doctor told Louis, who was gasping for breath on the examining table.

But Louis refused. "Doc, you don't understand," he said. "My whole life, my whole soul, my whole spirit is to bloooow that horn. I've got bookings arranged and the people are waiting for me. I got to do it!"[14]

He played the Waldorf gig with the understanding that he would go to the hospital afterward. During the first show, booking agent Joe Sully of the Glaser office noticed a reviewer for television in the audience and suggested to Louis that they tune in after the show to watch the review.

"The guy reviews the show and pans the s—— out of him," Sully recalled. "Which wasn't necessary; he didn't have to pan the s—— out of him." Armstrong listened in silence, clearly stunned by the harsh words. When the reviewer was finished, Louis turned from the TV set to Sully. "But you'll still book me, huh, Joe?" he asked.

108   Jazz critic James Collier writes: "After all the adula-
tion, the hit records, the performances for crowned
heads, after all the awards . . . so little faith did he
have in his own worth that he could be destroyed by
one hasty review tossed off by an obscure commenta-
tor and forgotten five minutes later by everybody who
heard it. It is a pathetic story . . . because the pain
Armstrong felt was real. Nothing he had done had finally healed that wound carved into him in
boyhood."[15]

After several weeks in intensive care in the hospital,
Louis went home. By July 5 he felt well enough to tell
Dr. Schiff he was ready to perform again and ask him
to get the All Stars together for a rehearsal. He died at
five-thirty the next morning, a month short of his seventieth birthday, of kidney failure caused by a failing
heart.

Armstrong's death was front-page news around
the world, and expressions of sorrow and affection
came from everywhere. A statement from U.S. president Richard Nixon spoke for many: "Mrs. Nixon and I
share the sorrow of millions of Americans at the death
of Louis Armstrong. One of the architects of an American art form, a free and individual spirit, and an artist
of worldwide fame, his great talents and magnificent
spirit added riches and pleasure to all our lives."

Some twenty-five thousand mourners filed past the
body as it lay in state in a National Guard armory in
New York, and the funeral the next day was covered
by national television. Honorary pallbearers included
such jazz personalities as Pearl Bailey, Ella Fitzgerald,
Frank Sinatra, Bing Crosby, and Dizzy Gillespie, as
well as celebrities from other branches of show business. At Lucille's request, Al Hibbler sang "Nobody
Knows the Trouble I've Seen" and "When the Saints
Go Marching In." There was no other music at the service except for a rendition of "The Lord's Prayer" by

singer Peggy Lee—although Louis reportedly would have liked a New Orleans jazz band. He did get one later, at a New Orleans memorial service attended by fifteen thousand people.

Louis Armstrong was gone, but Satchmo surely is here to stay. It is no exaggeration to describe him as the most influential American artist of the twentieth century, a creative giant whose work has been a model for generations of musicians. Preserved on records and tapes, his playing and singing will continue to bring pleasure and inspiration for centuries to come.

SOURCE NOTES

Chapter One

1. James Lincoln Collier, *The Making of Jazz* (Boston: Houghton Mifflin, 1978), p. 23.

2. Barry Ulanov, *A History of Jazz in America* (New York: Da Capo Press, 1972), p. 27.

3. *The Making of Jazz,* p. 63.

4. Ibid., p. 44.

5. Jack V. Buerkle and Danny Barker, *Bourbon Street Black* (New York: Oxford University Press, 1973), p. 63.

6. *The Making of Jazz,* p. 67.

7. Ibid., p. 58.

8. Dan Morgenstern, *Jazz People* (New York: Harry N. Abrams, 1976), p. 24.

9. Ramsey and Smith, eds., *Jazzmen* (New York: Harcourt, Brace, 1939), p. 12.

10. Alan Lomax, *Mr. Jelly Roll* (Berkeley: University of California Press, 1950), p. 84.

Chapter Two

1. Gary Giddins, *Satchmo* (New York: Doubleday, 1988), p. 48.

2. Louis Armstrong, *My Life in New Orleans* (New York: Prentice-Hall, 1954), quoted in *Satchmo*, p. 53.

3. Ibid., p. 57.

4. Ibid.

5. James Lincoln Collier, *The Making of Jazz* (Boston: Houghton Mifflin, 1978), p. 143.

6. *Satchmo*, p. 63.

7. Ibid., p. 62.

8. Ibid., p. 59.

9. Ibid., p. 64.

10. Ibid.

11. Rudi Blesh, *Shining Trumpets* (New York: Alfred Knopf, 1946), p. 172.

12. Barry Ulanov, *A History of Jazz in America* (New York: Da Capo Press, 1972), p. 71

13. *The Making of Jazz*, p. 143.

14. James Lincoln Collier, *Louis Armstrong—An American Genius* (New York: Oxford University Press, 1983), p. 66.

15. *A History of Jazz in America*, p. 71.

16. Hugues Panassie, *Louis Armstrong* (New York: Charles Scribner's Sons, 1971), p. 6.

17. *Satchmo*, p. 67.

18. Ibid.

Chapter Three

1. Barry Ulanov, *A History of Jazz in America* (New York: Da Capo Press, 1972), p. 73.

2. Louis Armstrong, *Swing That Music* (New York: Longmans, Green, 1936), p. 47.

112 3. Max Jones and John Chilton, *Louis* (London: November Books, 1971), p. 58.

4. Ibid.

5. Hugues Panassie, *Louis Armstrong* (New York: Charles Scribner's Sons, 1971), p. 9.

6. *Louis,* p. 58.

7. James Lincoln Collier, *The Making of Jazz* (Boston: Houghton Mifflin, 1978), p. 149.

8. Rudi Blesh, *Shining Trumpets* (New York: Alfred Knopf, 1946), p. 85.

9. Armstrong letter to Max Jones, quoted in *Louis,* p. 10.

10. *Louis,* p. 205.

11. Dan Morgenstern, *Jazz People* (New York: Harry N. Abrams, 1976), p. 85.

12. Fredric Ramsey in *Jazzmen,* quoted in *Louis,* p. 62.

13. Hoagy Carmichael, *The Stardust Road* (New York: Rinehart, 1946), p. 42.

14. James Lincoln Collier, *Louis Armstrong—An American Genius* (New York: Oxford University Press, 1983), p. 95.

15. *Louis,* p. 68.

16. Ibid., p. 69.

17. Robert Goffin, *Horn of Plenty* (New York: Allen Towne & Heath, 1947), quoted in Gary Giddins, *Satchmo* (New York: Doubleday, 1988), p. 79.

18. *Louis Armstrong—An American Genius,* p. 113.

19. *Louis,* p. 77.

Chapter Four

1. Max Jones and John Chilton, *Louis* (London: November Books, 1971), p. 83.

2. Ibid.

3. Whitney Balliett, *Such Sweet Thunder* (New York: Bobbs, Merrill, 1966), p. 295.

4. Robert Goffin, *Horn of Plenty* (New York: Allen Towne & **113**
Heath, 1947), p. 201.

5. *Louis,* p. 91.

6. Gary Giddins, *Satchmo* (New York: Doubleday, 1988), p.
85.

7. *Louis,* p. 92.

8. *Satchmo,* p. 79.

9. *Such Sweet Thunder,* p. 296.

10. Hugues Panassie, *Louis Armstrong* (New York: Charles
Scribner's Sons, 1971), p. 73.

11. Louis Armstrong, *Swing That Music* (New York: Longmans,
Green, 1936), p. 101.

12. Ibid., p. 85.

13. James Lincoln Collier, *Louis Armstrong—An American Genius* (New York: Oxford University Press, 1983), p. 223.

Chapter Five

1. Max Jones and John Chilton, *Louis* (London: November
Books, 1971), p. 102.

2. Ibid., p. 103.

3. Ibid., p. 113.

4. Ibid.

5. James Lincoln Collier, *Louis Armstrong—An American Genius* (New York: Oxford University Press, 1983), p. 224.

6. Louis Armstrong, *Swing That Music* (New York: Longmans,
Green, 1936), p. 96.

7. Gary Giddins, *Satchmo* (New York: Doubleday, 1988),
p. 126.

8. *Louis Armstrong—An American Genius,* p. 261.

9. Hugues Panassie, *Louis Armstrong* (New York: Charles
Scribner's Sons, 1971), p. 18.

10. *Louis Armstrong—An American Genius,* p. 273.

11. Ibid., p. 265.

114   Chapter Six

1.   James Lincoln Collier, *Louis Armstrong—An American Genius* (New York: Oxford University Press, 1983), p. 287.

2.   Ibid.

3.   Ibid., p. 235.

4.   Louis Armstrong, *Swing That Music* (New York: Longmans, Green, 1936), p. 74.

5.   Ibid., p. 123.

6.   *Louis Armstrong—An American Genius,* p. 274.

7.   Ibid.

8.   Pops Foster, *Pops Foster* (Berkeley: University of California Press, 1971), p. 159.

9.   *Harpers,* November 1967, quoted in *Louis Armstrong—An American Genius,* p. 277.

10.   *Louis Armstrong—An American Genius,* p. 289.

11.   Gary Giddins, *Satchmo* (New York: Doubleday, 1988), p. 138.

12.   *Louis Armstrong—An American Genius,* p. 278.

13.   Max Jones and John Chilton, *Louis* (London: November Books, 1971), p. 162.

14.   *Satchmo,* p. 146.

15.   *Louis,* p. 168.

16.   *Louis Armstrong—An American Genius,* p. 282.

17.   Ibid.

18.   *Satchmo,* p. 147.

Chapter Seven

1.   Barry Ulanov, *A History of Jazz in America* (New York: Da Capo Press, 1972), p. 78.

2.   Gary Giddins, *Satchmo* (New York: Doubleday, 1988), p. 156.

3. Ibid., p. 105.

4. Dan Morgenstern, *Jazz People* (New York: Harry N. Abrams, 1976), p. 97.

5. *Satchmo*, p. 168.

6. James Lincoln Collier, *Louis Armstrong—An American Genius* (New York: Oxford University Press, 1983), p. 315.

7. Max Jones and John Chilton, *Louis* (London: November Books, 1971), p. 172.

8. John S. Wilson, *The Transition Years* (New York: Appleton-Century Crofts, 1966), p. 111.

9. *Louis*, p. 215.

10. Ibid., pp. 206, 215.

11. *Satchmo*, p. 189.

12. Ibid., p. 159.

13. *Jazz People*, p. 89.

14. Whitney Balliett, *Such Sweet Thunder* (New York: Bobbs, Merrill, 1966), p. 297.

15. *Louis Armstrong—An American Genius*, pp. 245–246.

16. *Louis*, p. 180.

17. *Louis Armstrong—An American Genius*, p. 317.

18. *Louis*, p. 176.

19. *Jazz People*, p. 89.

20. Ibid.

21. *Louis*, p. 182.

22. Ibid., p. 183.

23. Ibid.

Chapter Eight

1. Max Jones and John Chilton, *Louis* (London: November Books, 1971), p. 246.

116   2.   Whitney Balliett, *Such Sweet Thunder* (New York: Bobbs, Merrill, 1966), p. 297.

3.   *Louis*, p. 191.

4.   James Lincoln Collier, *Louis Armstrong—An American Genius* (New York: Oxford University Press, 1983), p. 326.

5.   Ibid.

6.   Gary Giddins, *Satchmo* (New York: Doubleday, 1988), p. 189.

7.   Ibid., p. 197.

8.   *Louis Armstrong—An American Genius*, p. 325.

9.   *Louis*, p. 97.

10.   *Jet*, November 26, 1959, quoted in *Louis Armstrong—An American Genius*, p. 319.

11.   *Satchmo*, p. 203.

12.   *Louis Armstrong—An American Genius*, p. 328.

13.   *Satchmo*, pp. 14–20.

14.   *Louis Armstrong—An American Genius*, p. 331.

15.   Ibid., p. 332.

GLOSSARY

Arranger: A musician who adapts a composition to a particular style of performance through voices or instruments.

Bop (or bebop): An early form of modern jazz developed in the 1940s, notable for its chromatic and dissonant harmonies and its complex rhythms, which often obscure the melody line.

Brothel: A house of prostitution (also called bordello).

Cadenza: An elaborate flourish or showy musical passage, often improvised and played by an unaccompanied instrument during an orchestra piece.

Chromatic scale: A musical scale progressing entirely by halftones, with thirteen tones to the octave.

Falsetto: An artificial way of singing or talking in which the voice is used in a register much higher than that of its natural range.

118   Honky-tonk: (slang) A noisy, disreputable nightclub or dance hall.

Mute: A device placed in the bell of a brass instrument to soften or muffle its tone.

Ragtime: A type of American music especially popular between the years 1890 and 1915, which was characterized by strong syncopation in the melody and accompanied in strict two-four time.

Rhythm and blues: A music popular with urban blacks, which features a strong, repetitive beat and simple melodies. In the 1950s, a commercialized form of rhythm and blues developed into rock-and-roll.

Riff: A melodic phrase, often constantly repeated, which forms an accompaniment for a jazz soloist. *Riffing* by the brass or woodwind sections was a basic feature of the Big Band era.

Scat singing: Jazz singing in which meaningless syllables are improvised to take the place of words and often to imitate the sounds of instruments.

Syncopation: A shifting of the normal accent in musical rhythm, usually by stressing beats which are normally unaccented (also called *counterpoint*).

Uncle Tom: A black whose behavior toward whites is regarded as fawning or servile; a term derived from the main character in Harriet Beecher Stowe's 1852 antislavery novel, *Uncle Tom's Cabin*.

Vibrato: A pulsating effect produced by the rapid alternation of a musical tone with a slight variation in pitch.

FOR FURTHER READING

Basie, Count and Albert Murray. *Good Morning Blues: The Autobiography of Count Basie.* New York: Random House, 1985.

Chilton, John. *Sidney Bechet, the Wizard of Jazz.* New York: Oxford University Press, 1987.

Collier, James L. *Duke Ellington.* New York: Oxford University Press, 1987.

Collier, James L. *Louis Armstrong, an American Success Story.* New York: Macmillan, 1985.

Collier, James L. *The Great Jazz Artists.* New York: Four Winds Press, 1977.

Cornell, Jean Gay. *Louis Armstrong—Ambassador Satchmo.* Champaign, Ill.: Garrard Publishing Co., 1972.

120 Giddins, Gary. *Satchmo.* New York: Doubleday, 1988.

Hentoff, Nat. *Journey Into Jazz.* New York: Coward, 1968.

Hughes, Langston. *The First Book of Jazz.* 3rd edition. New York: Franklin Watts, 1982.

Hughes, Langston. *Famous Negro Music Makers.* New York: Dodd, 1955.

Longstreet, Stephen. *Storyville to Harlem: Fifty years on the jazz scene.* New Brunswick, N.J.: Rutgers Univ. Press, 1986.

Myrus, Donald. *I Like Jazz.* New York: Macmillan, 1964.

Neil, Leonard. *Jazz and the White Americans: The acceptance of a new art form.* Chicago: University of Chicago Press, 1962.

Schafer, William J. *Brass Bands and New Orleans Jazz.* Baton Rouge, La.: Louisiana State University Press, 1977.

Wilmer, Valerie. *As Serious As Your Life: The story of the new jazz.* London/New York: Quartet Books, 1977.

INDEX